Discrimination

Prejudice in Action

Scott Gillam

—Multicultural Issues—

ENSLOW PUBLISHERS, INC.

44 Fadem Rd.	P.O. Box 38
Box 699	Aldershot
Springfield, N.J. 07081	Hants GU12 6BP
U.S.A.	U.K.

For Molly, Timothy, and Jonathon

Library of Congress Cataloging-in-Publication Data

Gillam, Scott
    Discrimination: prejudice in action / Scott Gillam.
        p. cm. — (Multicultural Issues)
    Includes bibliographical references and index.
    Summary: Examines the history, background, and societal
ramifications of discrimination and cites possible ways to deal with
discrimination and its consequences.
    ISBN 0-89490-643-7
    1. Discrimination—United States—Juvenile literature.
2. Prejudices—United States—Juvenile literature. 3. Minorities—
United States—Juvenile literature. [1. Discrimination.
2. Prejudices.] I. Title. II. Series.
HN90.S6G55   1995
303.3'85—dc20   94-38962
                                                    CIP
                                                    AC

Printed in the United States of America.

10 9 8 7 6 5 4 3 2 1

Photo Credits: Andrew Lichtenstein/Impact Visuals, p. 57; Don Vendeventer, p.
46; Jerome Friar/Impact Visuals, p. 34; Jetta Fraser/Impact Visuals, p. 97; Linda
Eber/Educators for Social Responsibility, p. 37; Marco Vega, p. 74; New York
Public Library, p. 14; Robert Fox/Impact Visuals, p. 103; United States Supreme
Court, p. 7; Xerox Imaging Systems, p. 81.

Cover Photo: Photo Edit/Michael Newman

Contents

Discrimination in Action

In the summer of 1954 the author of this book, a white New Yorker, was a teenager traveling by train across South Carolina. He was with his older cousin, a white native of Georgia. The two had wearily walked through most of the train's cars, looking for an empty seat. Finally the author found one and started to sit down, but his cousin motioned not to. "Negro car," he whispered.

Then the author realized that, in fact, every face in that car was black, while every face in the previous cars had been white. As strange as it sounds today, the laws of the United States in the 1950s permitted segregation—the separation of different races or ethnic groups—not only in schools, but also on buses and other public accommodations.

How would you feel if your seat on a train or bus were determined by the color of your skin?

▼ ▼ ▼

In 1960 the Dean of Harvard Law School suggested to Felix Frankfurter, a United States Supreme Court Justice, that he hire one of his best students, Ruth Bader Ginsburg, as a law clerk. The Justice replied that he was not ready to hire a woman. Resolving to devote her life to obtaining better career choices for women, Ginsburg went on to become a distinguished women's advocate and federal judge. In 1993, President Bill Clinton nominated Ruth Bader Ginsburg to the United States Supreme Court. Ginsburg became the second woman ever appointed to the Supreme Court.[1]

How would you react if you were told that despite your great qualifications, you couldn't be hired because you were the wrong gender?

▼ ▼ ▼

In 1993 James Dale, a twenty-one-year-old college student and former Eagle Scout, sued the Boy Scouts of America. He said his membership in the organization had been canceled after the Scouts found out that he was gay. "I owe it to the organization to point out to them how bad and wrong this policy [of excluding gays] is. Being proud of who I am is something the Boy Scouts taught me. They taught me to stand up for what I believe in."

Blake Lewis, a spokesperson for the Boy Scouts, said, "We don't think a homosexual presents a role model that's consistent with the expectations of mainstream American families."[2]

Nominated by President Bill Clinton in 1993, Ruth Bader Ginsburg is only the second woman to become a United States Supreme Court Justice.

In 1991, however, the Boy Scouts did start a new program—called "Learning for Life"—that admits gay members, atheists, and girls. The program is the first scout-related curriculum to openly include gay members. The curriculum, however, is separate from the usual scout programs. And the program is only directed by local scout councils that choose to offer it. Gay men are still not permitted to be scoutmasters, and the separate program for gay scouts has been criticized as a "second-class program" that does not send a healthy psychological message.[3]

If you were gay, do you think that a separate program for Boy Scouts like yourself would help you feel proud? Or do you think such a program would make you feel like a second-class scout?

▼ ▼ ▼

When Stevie Wonder was born blind in 1950, his parents might have thought he would always be dependent upon other people to support him for the rest of his life. Many people assume that when a person has a disability, he or she must live a very limited life. A disability may be physical, such as blindness or deafness, or mental, such as retardation. Sometimes people without disabilities react to persons with disabilities as if the latter are totally helpless instead of observing how independent those with disabilities may actually be.

Fortunately, Stevie Wonder's parents chose to encourage their son to develop his great gift for music. By the age of thirteen "Little Stevie Wonder" had already recorded his first No. 1 hit record—a live rhythm and blues song called "Fingertips, Part 2." Through the years Stevie Wonder—now no longer "Little"—has written and performed dozens of hit songs, including "Uptight (Everything's Alright)," "You Are the Sunshine of My Life," "I Ain't Gonna Stand for It," "Love Light in Flight," and "Go-Home." In 1988 Stevie Wonder was elected to the Rock and Roll Hall of Fame.[4]

If you had been Stevie Wonder's parent, would you have settled for less than a full life for your child?

▼▼▼

In 1991 Hardee Food Systems, a fast food chain, fired more than two thousand workers under the age of sixteen across the country. The reason? Hardee officials said a federal crackdown on child labor laws made it too risky to employ fourteen- and fifteen-year-olds. Federal law prohibits such youths from working past 7 P.M. on school nights. The Maryland Human Relations Commission, however, did not accept the explanation given by Hardee officials. The commission sued Hardee Food Systems for violating Maryland's age discrimination law by unfairly penalizing the teenagers.[5]

Do you think that Hardee Food Systems acted fairly in the across-the-board firings? Or were company officials just taking what they thought was the safest way out of a possible lawsuit for even unintentional violations of child labor laws?

At some time in your life you may have faced a situation similar to one of those described in the preceding paragraphs. Perhaps you were rejected from doing some job. Maybe you resented being left out of a certain group. Perhaps you were forbidden from going somewhere that you really wanted to go because of something about your background or capabilities that you could do nothing about. Sometimes such an experience leaves scars that can last a lifetime.

In this book you will meet people in many walks of life who have felt rejected or discriminated against. Like those African Americans riding that train through South Carolina, you may be a victim of racial discrimination. Like Ruth Bader Ginsburg, you may suffer from discrimination because of your gender. Like James Dale, you may feel excluded because you are homosexual. Like Stevie Wonder, you may be subject to discrimination because you have a disability. Or like the teenaged fast-food workers at Hardee restaurants, you may be fired because you fall into a certain age group. Yet like these people, you too, can learn how to fight discrimination and reverse its vicious circle.

In this book you will learn what discrimination is. You will find out more about the different kinds of discrimination and how they have developed over the years. You will learn about laws that have been passed to make it harder to discriminate against others. And you will meet individuals and groups that have successfully fought discrimination in each of its forms. Welcome to the struggle for human rights!

Defining Discrimination

When the author of this book was about ten years old, a new family with two children moved into his neighborhood. The author's family lived near a university, and the father of the new family had been hired to teach in one of the departments there. José was about the author's age and Lisa was a year or two older. Both José and Lisa spoke English, but José's accent made him difficult to understand at first. In addition, he was a big broad-shouldered boy who may have appeared clumsy, even though he wasn't.*

One afternoon a group of neighborhood boys was playing in the park. A disagreement with José arose over something—the author has long since forgotten what. What the author does remember is that the group of boys chased José home, calling him names.

*The names have been changed to protect privacy.

José's foreign origin was the focus of the group's taunts. "Go back where you came from!" rang the jeers. The author remembers feeling that he and his friends were doing something terribly wrong. Yet, somehow, he was unable to separate himself from the group. Why? Perhaps because the actions of the group of boys seemed so angry, the author feared what would happen to him if he expressed his feelings.

Fortunately, this particular incident was part of a story that ended happily. Gradually José and Lisa were accepted into the community. José became popular among the boys who had taunted him, and Lisa was eventually elected president of a local youth group.

Many stories like this, however, do not end so happily. Later in this chapter we will examine the different types of discrimination to be discussed in this book. But first, a few definitions.

The group's act of discrimination against José was based on stereotypes. A stereotype is a fixed and oversimplified mental picture of a group of people that doesn't account for individual differences. In the preceding case, the group rejected José only because he fit its stereotype of a foreigner.

In focusing on this stereotype, the group of boys did not consider that, as a newcomer to the United States, José couldn't be expected to speak the language perfectly or to know his way around. José was a really nice person when you got to know him. By focusing only on the stereotype of José as a foreigner, however, the boys kept themselves from seeing José as a person.

Stereotypes are usually the basis of prejudice. Prejudice refers to a negative attitude or an opinion, formed beforehand, that a person holds about some individual, group, or object.

Another word for prejudice is bias, or the tendency to favor one side over another. Most people would regard calling José names as an example of prejudice.

Discrimination means acting unfavorably toward someone based on the group to which that person belongs rather than on the person's own merits. In other words, when you discriminate, you don't consider the person as a person, but only as a stereotype. Prejudice is a belief or attitude. Discrimination involves an action. By chasing José home, the boys were discriminating against him.

Unfortunately, people's brains often use stereotyped thinking to help quickly sort large amounts of information. For example, faced with a huge bag of what looks like vegetables and fruits, we may describe them only as "things to eat," since we don't recognize all the fruit-like or vegetable-like foods in the bag. Similarly, when we are faced with a red-haired person whom we have never met, we may be tempted to think of that person according to some stereotype of red-haired people. We may believe that all redheads are hot-tempered or flirts or whatever. Only by talking to the person can we get beyond the stereotype and discover who that person really is.

Discrimination Against Race or Cultural Group

The word race has been used to refer to a group of human beings who have passed on certain physical

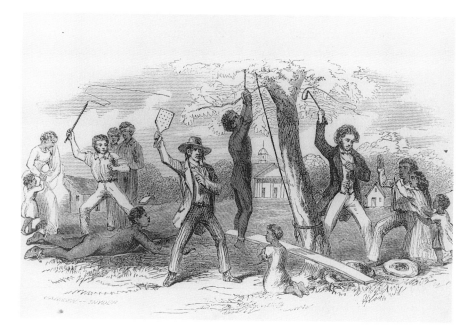

In the United States, discrimination against African Americans has existed for hundreds of years. Its roots can be traced as far back as 1619 when Africans were brought here against their will to serve as indentured servants.

characteristics—skin color, eye shape, and other such traits—from one generation to another. Since people from the traditionally designated races have tended to intermingle over time, however, it generally makes little sense to talk of race in the traditional sense. A more useful concept in defining large groups of people whose identity has persisted over time is culture. Culture can be defined as the sum total of the ways of living built up by a group of human beings and passed on from one generation to another.

Discrimination because of race or culture is common throughout the world. For example, in the United States discrimination against African Americans began soon after the earliest African immigrants arrived at Jamestown in 1619. They were brought against their will as indentured servants, who were supposed to earn their freedom by working for their masters over a period of years. Some whites were also indentured servants. By a series of laws, however, the British rulers of Virginia gradually took away the rights of African Americans and made them slaves. Slaves had no legal rights and were considered the property of their owners. This treatment of a people is an example of racism, or the belief that one race or culture—usually one's own—is superior to all others.

Slavery, an example of racism and legal discrimination on a national scale, continued for over two hundred years until President Abraham Lincoln issued the Emancipation Proclamation in 1863, during the middle of the Civil War. In 1865, Congress ratified the Thirteenth Amendment, which abolished slavery. Despite these legal safeguards, discrimination against African Americans has persisted into the twentieth century. This persistence has made necessary later laws such as the Federal Civil Rights Act of 1964, the Voting Rights Act of 1965, and many other anti-discriminatory measures.

In Chapter 3 you will read how race has divided peoples and how some individuals and groups have overcome this barrier.

Gender Bias

In Chapter 1, you read how Ruth Bader Ginsburg was unable to get a job as a lawyer when she first graduated from law school in 1960 because of discrimination against women. Many strides toward equality for women in the job market have been made since then. Many signs of gender discrimination still remain, however, not only in the workplace but in society in general.

Why should there be discrimination against women in the first place? There are actually about 2 percent more women born into the world than men. Women also live longer. Some anthropologists—scientists who study the origin, development, races, customs, and beliefs of human beings—have made a strong case for the natural superiority of women. The issue of gender discrimination is complicated. People sometimes disagree on whether a particular case actually involves discrimination against women or simply recognizes built-in differences between the two sexes.

In Chapter 4 we will consider discrimination against

women not only in the workplace but also in the classroom, school sports, and various consumer situations.

Discrimination Against Gays and Lesbians

Many people today believe that being homosexual, having sexual feeling for a person of the same sex, is a result of a genetic trait. Most studies indicate that around 13 percent of adult males and 7 percent of adult females, or an average of 10 percent of the total population, are homosexual.[1] Today the terms "gay" for men and women and "lesbian" for women are considered to be respectful ways of referring to homosexuals.

Awareness of homosexuals by society has probably been increased by society's concern with the current epidemic of AIDS, which stands for Acquired Immune Deficiency Syndrome. AIDS leaves the body's immune system unable to resist serious infection. HIV, the virus that causes AIDS, is spread through intimate sexual contact, contaminated needles used to inject drugs, or from an infected mother to her unborn child. HIV, the Human Immunodeficiency Virus, is transmitted through blood. Before reliable tests for screening blood were developed, blood transfusions were another major route of transmission. Male homosexuals were the first group in the United States to be widely infected by the disease, which was first identified in New York in 1979. Some political conservatives and fundamentalist religious leaders have condemned gay men and women as deserving victims of their own immoral practices or as sinners being punished by God. Most of the gay population has increased the practice of "safe sex." The disease, however, has spread to other groups, including drug-users and heterosexuals. The HIV infection is currently growing fastest among heterosexuals, both in the United States and throughout the world. Some people, however, mistakenly continue to think of the HIV virus and AIDS as diseases of homosexuals and drug addicts.[2]

Despite increased awareness and acceptance of gays and lesbians, many people still harbor suspicions and fears about them. Some of these people base their attitudes on religious beliefs. Others are prejudiced against gays and lesbians as "different" just as they are prejudiced against other minorities. Still others say they are not prejudiced against homosexuals; they just don't think school children are old enough to discuss the subject of homosexuality. Many of these people may also disapprove of school sex education courses in general, unless the courses focus only on reproductive biology and abstinence, or refraining from sexual intercourse.

No one would disagree that discrimination against homosexuals, for whatever reasons, remains widespread. In Chapter 5 you will read about the history of the gay and lesbian rights movement, and the efforts being made to combat discrimination against homosexuals.

Age Discrimination

Chances are you don't think about getting old at all; it's simply not on your agenda. This fact is not so surprising. For you, as a teenager, there are many other important issues to think about—such as why your body seems to be growing the way it does and just who that face in the mirror really belongs to.

You might think about this fact, though: Of all the groups against whom discrimination is most commonly practiced, older people are the one group to which you have an almost 100 percent chance of eventually belonging. As unlikely as it sounds, you too, will probably grow old. And if science keeps coming up with new ways to prolong life, you'll probably live longer than your parents.

Just how should we define *old?* Like so many terms, the definition depends on the context. "You're as old as you feel," says an eighty-year-old great-grandfather as he takes off on his daily two-mile walk. In many universities, professors need not retire until the age of seventy or even older. In most businesses, however, *old* is defined as the age of sixty-five, when company employees must usually retire. In some companies, however, employees may elect retirement as early as fifty-five.

When you become old, whenever that is, you may be fortunate enough to retire from your job and live comfortably, surrounded by loving friends and family. Or you may find yourself poor and alone. Most likely you'll find yourself somewhere in between. In any case, however, you will probably at some point be discriminated against simply because you are a certain age.

Why do people discriminate against people because of

their age? As in most cases of discrimination, it's usually a matter of ignorance. In Chapter 6 we will examine the various forms that age discrimination can take, both on and off the job, against the old and the young alike. We'll also see how age discrimination is being fought by various groups as well as by new laws.

Discrimination Against People with Disabilities

When you see someone in a wheelchair, chances are that at least a part of you inwardly says, "Thank God that's not me." This response suggests that on some level you recognize that person *could have been* you. Like older persons, people with disabilities are a group that will probably some day include a great majority of us. To be exact, the chances are seven out of ten that you will at some point in your life have a partial or total disability.[3] This truth in itself may help to explain why some people discriminate against those with disabilities. Precisely because many of us may someday have a partial or total disability, we react by trying to distance ourselves from the situation. We tell ourselves that this can't possibly happen to us.

Unfortunately this kind of behavior, since it is based on a stereotype with only a grain of truth, leads to a dishonest kind of life based on illusions rather than reality. In real life we all face challenges whether we have a disability or not. All of us, each in our own way, want to live a life in which we don't have to depend on others. Perhaps thinking along those lines will help us identify more with the situation of people with disabilities and realize that in many ways we are really quite similar.

Physical disabilities include loss of part or all of one or more of the senses. For example, a person may be totally or partially blind, or totally or partially deaf, or both. A person may have a partial or total loss of some physical capability—such as the need for crutches to support one's legs and feet, or a wheelchair to support one's lower body; a speech problem; difficulty in using one's hands or arms; or a combination of these conditions. But note that all of these conditions affect one's body; they do not mean that the person with a physical disability will also have a mental disability.

On the other hand, there are people who have a mental disability without being physically disabled in any way. Some of these people have a learning disability or a lower IQ than is considered normal. Others may have a mental condition—schizophrenia, depression, or autism—that can be controlled by medication or psychotherapy. Many of these individuals can lead normal lives; all can still make a contribution to society. Yet they suffer discrimination for many of the same reasons that persons with physical disabilities do.

In Chapter 7, you will read about the many efforts to aid and protect those with physical or mental disabilities from discrimination, whether in schooling and jobs or in physical access with respect to these and other areas.

The Vicious Circle of Discrimination

What do all these types of discrimination—based on race or cultural group, gender, sexual orientation, age, or ability—have in common? In each case, the individuals being discriminated against are kept from taking their full place in society as individuals by the actions of prejudiced people. As a result of discrimination, racial minorities and women have lower salaries than whites, and older workers are laid off first. The fact that those discriminated against now occupy "inferior" places in society as a result of discrimination gives additional support to those who were prejudiced against them in the first place. Prejudice and discrimination by whites and the low economic status of blacks, for example, thus could be said to "cause" each other. As long as white discrimination continues, blacks will continue to have low economic status. A "vicious circle," as described by Gunnar Myrdal, is set up in the following way. A negative action by prejudiced whites against blacks automatically produces a negative reaction by blacks, which in turn only increases white prejudice toward blacks, and so on. If nothing is done to reverse this vicious circle, and discrimination becomes worse, the eventual result can be social disunity.[4]

If, however, white discrimination against blacks, for example, is decreased, this positive development can increase black economic status, which in turn can further lessen white discrimination, and so on. In this way the vicious circle is reversed. In fact, according to Myrdal's theory, just as the downward spiral gets much worse as it goes on in the same direction, so the reversed circle gets much better as it goes in a positive upward direction.[5]

How does discrimination begin and grow? What can we do to slow, halt, or reverse its growth? We will examine these questions as we take a closer look at each of the major groups affected by discrimination.

Racial Discrimination

Although African Americans make up 13 percent of the population, they are found in less than 1 percent of the upper management positions in large businesses.

▼ ▼ ▼

A white pedestrian ignores a black pedestrian's request for directions for fear that the black person may be a panhandler or worse.

▼ ▼ ▼

A middle class housing complex sets racial quotas that restrict the number of minority tenants.

▼ ▼ ▼

A Hispanic student is placed in a slower-paced class at school, even though her intelligence tests show her to be above average in ability.

▼ ▼ ▼

A white pre-med student sues a university that failed to admit him to medical school, even though he had a higher grade-point average than some minority students who were admitted.

▲ ▲ ▲

These examples show that racial discrimination occurs in many situations—on the job, on the street, in housing, and in schools. It also occurs among almost every racial and cultural group—whites, blacks, Asians, Europeans, and Americans. However, racial minorities are usually the victims of discrimination, while whites are usually the perpetrators.

Racial discrimination exists in the United States despite a series of laws passed years ago to discourage it. In the famous *Brown* v. *Board of Education* decision in 1954, the United States Supreme Court declared segregation in schools to be unconstitutional. Previously, "separate but equal" schools had been legal under the *Plessy* v. *Ferguson* decision of 1896.

In 1957 Congress passed the first civil rights law to protect black voting rights since the Reconstruction period that followed the Civil War. In 1961 President Kennedy issued Executive Order 10925. It required that industries fulfilling government contracts "take affirmative action to ensure that applicants are employed, and that employees are treated during employment without regard to their race, creed, color, or national origin." Later, the order was extended to include gender as well.[1]

Affirmative action means taking active steps to seek out

minority and women applicants for jobs instead of waiting for people in these categories to apply. This concept has continued to be an employment policy into the 1990s, with some setbacks. The Civil Rights Act of 1964 banned discrimination in voting, jobs, and public accommodations. The Voting Rights Act of 1965 further extended voting rights for blacks. Also in 1965 the national origins quota system of immigration was banned.[2]

In spite of these achievements, however, discrimination is not only widespread, but may actually be increasing. One measure of this increase is the number of hate crimes reported.

The Federal Government published the first data on hate crimes in January 1993, in response to the Hate Crimes Statistics Act of 1990. A hate crime is a crime committed against an individual or group because of actual or perceived race, religion, ethnic origin, or sexual orientation. A total of 4,558 hate crimes were reported in 1991. Intimidation accounted for one-third of all offenses, followed by vandalism and assault. Anti-black offenses accounted for 36 percent of the total, followed by anti-white (19 percent) and anti-Jewish (17 percent). One national survey found that between the years 1989 and 1992, hate-related cross-burnings doubled, hate-related vandalism tripled, and racially- or ethnically-related murders and assaults increased significantly.[3]

Racial Discrimination: The Sounds of Silence

Why is racial discrimination still present despite so many efforts to combat it? One answer is that the kind of discrimination most common today is often more subtle and, therefore, harder to combat than the obvious types once seen.

John Dovidio is a psychologist who has studied modern acts of racism, or the belief that one racial or cultural group—usually one's own—is superior to all others. Dovidio has identified five characteristics of what he calls "aversive" racism, or racism that is expressed by avoiding people of other races or interracial situations. According to Dovidio, typical aversive racists:

1. Say they are in favor of equal treatment of all groups, at least in theory.
2. Try to avoid interracial situations because of unconscious negative feelings toward other races.
3. Feel uncomfortable rather than actively hateful when experiencing interracial interaction.
4. Behave strictly according to established rules of social behavior in an interracial situation, and often claim that color plays no part in their behavior.
5. Express negative feelings about another race only in subtle ways that they can rationalize or justify to themselves.[4]

To test these characteristics, Dovidio ran experiments involving interracial situations in a laboratory setting. For example, to show how whites rationalize their anti-black feelings, he created a situation in which either a black or a white was the victim of a serious accident. When a white subject was told that he or she was the only witness to the accident, the subject helped black and white victims equally as often.

However, when a white witness was told that there were two other witnesses to the accident, the white witness helped black victims only half as often as he or she helped white victims. The white witness was able to rationalize his or her discrimination by stating the belief that one of the two other witnesses would help instead.[5]

Looking at Institutional Racism

When an established organization uses its power to favor one race over another, a situation called institutional racism exists. The policies and practices of institutions are set by individuals. Since some, perhaps many, of these individuals have racist feelings—however well hidden—it is not surprising that institutions in which such people have power will enforce racist policies or practices—however subtly or unconsciously.

Banks, which often lend people money to buy homes, are one place where institutional racism can occur. A study was made by the Boston Federal Reserve Bank of 4,000 loan applications to 131 banks in the Boston area in 1990. The study found that blacks and Hispanics were 60 percent more likely to be turned down for home loans than whites with similar financial backgrounds. Race was not the most important factor; a past bankruptcy or a previous home loan rejection were much more frequent reasons for being rejected. Yet race was the third most important reason for being turned down for a home loan.[6]

Two solutions have been proposed to deal with this

problem. The bankers themselves think that sensitivity training will help. But some consumer groups would rather go further. They favor strengthening the law, which now requires only that banks disclose their minority lending records.[7]

Even agencies of the U.S. government have been sources of institutional racism. The Immigration and Naturalization Service (INS) controls the flow of immigrants to the United States. In 1993 *U.S. News & World Report* investigated INS. The magazine found that only about 12 percent of INS employees were black—a lower percent than most other federal police agencies. Even more serious, none of INS's fifty-six branch offices was headed by a black, and no blacks had ever been promoted to the senior-level office corps. Not suprisingly, discrimination complaints within the agency rose from 39 in 1988 to 139 in 1992. One black INS investigator applied for more than seventy promotions over a three-year period. Although rated qualified for every single job, he was chosen for none. It is uncertain whether INS can reform itself or whether its problems will have to be settled in court.[8]

Case Studies in Lessening Racial Discrimination

To curb both outright and aversive racism, individual and institutional racism, a variety of strategies are needed. Let's look at some broad approaches and specific success stories. Approaches that have proved helpful involve individual action, legal action, broad-based study and action, and sensitivity training.

Individual Action: Marsing High School

Sometimes the efforts of just one or two people are enough to set back discrimination. Here's one example from the many described in *It's Our World, Too! Stories of Young People Who Are Making a Difference,* by Phillip Hoose.

Ernest "Neto" Villareal was one of ten Hispanic players on the Marsing High School football team in Idaho. He was tired of having white fans yell words aimed at Mexican Americans on the team whenever they made a mistake on the field.

Neto and his friend Jesse decided to call a meeting of the whole team. They discussed the problem, and at first unanimously voted not to play the next game as a protest against racism. Then all but four of the football players changed their mind. They decided football meant too much to them, and they would play despite the prejudiced comments.

Neto thought that if the fans knew why some players were quitting, perhaps they could change their behavior. He decided to ask the student council president, Andy Percifield, a tall red-haired senior, for help. Andy agreed to draft a letter from the students asking everyone at the next football game to take a stand against prejudice. The letter asked school authorities to eject any spectator who made prejudiced remarks.

Andy called a special meeting of the student council and the entire student body. He read a draft of the letter and asked for comments. After making a few changes, the student body unanimously approved the letter. The four football players who had decided not to play were so impressed with this vote of support that they changed their minds and decided to play in the next game.

Neto also asked a Hispanic teacher named Baldimar Elizondo for advice. Mr. Elizondo told Neto to take his complaint directly to the local school board, which was meeting that night. Neto, accompanied by Mr. Elizondo, did speak to the school board. The school board members listened respectfully, but they didn't say they would do anything.

Then the school principal refused Andy permission to read the letter at halftime. Andy had only one choice left if he wanted to work within school channels. Accompanied by Mr. Elizondo, Andy took his case to the school superintendent, the top official in the school district. The school superintendent agreed with Andy's letter.

At the next game, the letter was distributed to every car entering the parking lot. It was also read by a student council member at halftime. The response: first silence, then cheers. Everyone stood up and clapped. A corner in race relations had been turned.

No anti-Mexican-American comments have been heard at games since the letter was read. However, people aren't kidding themselves; racial prejudice itself has not been wiped out at Marsing.

Yet, says Neto, "At least we made it known that we wouldn't accept racism in our school or from our fans. We made a difference in the part of our lives that we really could control."[9]

Legal Action: Denny's Restaurants

Beginning early in 1993 at different branches of Denny's restaurants, many groups of black customers—including families, young people, and even a group of black Secret Service agents—filed discrimination lawsuits against the nationwide chain. The suits claimed that a specific restaurant had either given the black customers very slow service, added a $2 cover charge, demanded prepayment for all meals, or actually denied them service, while treating white customers with respect.

In response, Denny's denied the charge of discrimination. The restaurant chain did agree, however, to strengthen its policies of equal treatment and to communicate those policies to all employees. Denny's also began working with Charles Davis, a local National Association of Colored People (NAACP) official in San Jose, California, to help set up a program to fight racial discrimination at Denny's. In a formal agreement worked out with the NAACP, Denny's agreed to:

1. Double the number of Denny's restaurants owned by blacks by 1997.
2. Add 325 minority managers to all operations of Flagstar, Denny's parent company, by 2001.
3. Add $1 billion in purchases from minority vendors by the same year.[10]
4. Pay more than $54 million to thousands of black customers who were refused services, had to wait for long periods for service, or who had to pay more than white patrons.[11]

Because a few people worked through the legal system, Denny's is now an example of progress, rather than problems, in race relations.

Broad-Based Study and Action: Sports and Society

The Center for the Study of Sport in Society is located at Northeastern University in Massachusetts. One task the center performs is to collect statistics on the numbers of minorities at the various levels of amateur and professional sports in the United States.

Baseball fans may recall two recent examples of racial discrimination in the management levels of major league baseball. In one example, the then vice-president of the Los Angeles Dodgers, Al Campanis, commented that the reason there weren't more African Americans at the manager level in baseball was perhaps that they did not have "some of the necessities" for the job. Campanis soon announced his early retirement from the Dodger management. The prejudice he revealed, however, is probably more widespread than many will admit.[12]

Similarly, Marge Schott, owner of the Cincinnati Reds, once commonly used racial slurs in referring to her players. She was fined and officially chastised for her behavior. Yet there are probably others at her level in sports who still *think* what she had the bad judgment to *say*. That is, they are prejudiced, though they don't actively discriminate.

By collecting its statistics on racial integration of professional

Approximately two hundred protesters, including the Reverend Jesse Jackson, picketed outside Oriole Park at Camden Yards in Baltimore where an all-star baseball game was being played in 1993. The group of protesters was challenging professional baseball's discriminatory hiring and promotion practices.

sports, the center has confirmed what most fans already sense. For the most part, sports teams are well integrated at the player level; yet at the management levels—coaches, umpires, managers, and owners—there is still room for improvement.

The truth is that sports—at all age and ability levels—can be an important arena for racial progress. One poll commissioned by the center showed that 70 percent of all high school students said they had become friends with someone from a different racial or ethnic group through playing sports. Among whites, the majority was 68 percent; among blacks, 77 percent; and among Hispanics, 79 percent. However, the same poll of high school students had some sobering figures about race relations in general:

- 57 percent said they had seen or heard a racial act involving violence either very often (21 percent) or occasionally (36 percent).

- 25 percent said they had personally been the victim of a racial incident, including 55 percent of all black high school students.[13]

How can baseball, just to take one example, be a means of lessening racial tension and discrimination? One way is to increase minority attendance at major league baseball parks. Many major league baseball stadiums are located in or near inner cities. Yet minority attendance at games, especially by African Americans, has been declining. Why? A study of baseball's original sixteen teams may show one reason. Ten of these teams moved between 1950 and 1970 from neighborhoods with an average of 49 percent black population to neighborhoods that were just 16 percent black. To help baseball rebuild its popularity in these areas, major league baseball started RBI (Reviving Baseball in Inner Cities). The program now reaches more than 10,000 inner-city players across the nation. The first RBI World Series was played in 1993 at Busch Stadium in St. Louis, Missouri. In a similar move, Coca-Cola's Homers for America program donated $645,000 in 1993 to help rebuild inner city sandlot ball fields.[14]

Fighting Discrimination in the Classroom

As we saw in the case of Neto Villareal and Andy Percifield, one of the best places to begin to attack discrimination is in school. Young people can often be more open to change than adults. Organizations such as the Anti-Defamation League (ADL), Educators for Social Responsibility in New York City, and the Southern Poverty Law Center in Montgomery, Alabama, run anti-discrimination programs in schools throughout the United States.

One popular program created by the ADL is called A World of Difference. It attacks discrimination in a variety of ways, including special television programs and public service announcements, teacher training workshops, and classroom-ready teacher resource materials.

These students are taking part in a role-playing exercise developed by Educators for Social Responsibility as a way of understanding each other better. Such activities help to combat discrimination both in and out of the classroom.

The purposes of the programs are to:

1. Build self-esteem, the valuing of oneself.
2. Develop critical thinking skills to tell the difference between reality and demagoguery (the practice of stirring up a person by appealing to their emotions and prejudices).
3. Combat stereotyping by providing examples of people who contradict stereotypes.
4. Build empathy (the act of experiencing the feelings of another person) with those who are different from us through use of literature, videos, or role playing.
5. Encourage participants to take active steps toward creating social justice, in order to counter the effects of prejudice throughout the world.[15]

These are large goals, indeed. Yet they are built on a solid foundation of research and experience in combating prejudice and discrimination. For example, much evidence indicates that low self-esteem is often a cause of discrimination. If you do not think well of yourself, you may try to blame someone else for your feelings of self-hatred or rejection. By encouraging students to take pride in themselves and by valuing each person's different background, the ADL program seeks to develop "confident individuals who do not need to prove themselves by putting down others."[16]

In addition to helping students value themselves, the program helps them value others. Whether we react to those who are different from us with curiosity and an open mind or with fear and scorn depends on how we have been taught to respond. By learning to see the similarities as well as the differences between ourselves and others, the ADL program helps people to "move beyond 'tolerating' differences to recognizing how these differences enrich our lives."[17]

Finally, the program teaches students to "recognize prejudice and injustice, and encourages them to take action to repair an imperfect world." By discussing disputed issues and taking action, all with the goal of seeking the common good, students develop an "increased confidence in their judgment and in their ability to have a positive effect upon the world around them." As one eighth-grade student wrote in an essay on prejudice:

> *No one is free of prejudice. We are all vulnerable. It is up to each of us to stamp it out. Division weakens us. Our strength lies in unity. Together, we can accomplish anything.*[18]

How much does it take to change from a prejudiced person into an unprejudiced one? Sometimes all it takes is a one-day workshop to start the process of change. Here is what one high school senior wrote after taking such a workshop:

> *I'm prejudiced. It's not something I'm proud of. It's not even something I usually think about. But I do know that it is something I want to change....Yes, I'm prejudiced. I have opinions I can't justify. But now I can admit this, and know that it doesn't have to be like that. I walked into that workshop prejudiced, and I walked out prejudiced, but knowing a little more about myself and my friends. It would be impossible to say that a one-day workshop really changed me that much—but it's a start.*[19]

chapter

4

Gender Discrimination

Suppose you are a girl, and a boy makes a suggestive remark to you. How can you tell if he is only flirting or if he is trying to torment you? Flirting is a kind of lighthearted or playful romance. However, if someone repeatedly bothers you because of your gender, that's sexual harassment, and it's against federal law.

The difference is important. If you like the other person and enjoy the attention, that's a very different feeling from not liking the person and feeling embarrassed or uncomfortable because of his or her remarks. Sexual harassment is serious. "The harassment may prevent children from choosing certain activities or classes," according to one expert. "Sexual harassment may poison the environment, reinforcing the idea that school isn't a safe or a just place."[1]

Sexual harassment is a form of gender discrimination, which is defined by one authority in the field as "preventing people from holding certain jobs or establishing different laws for different people solely on the basis of sex..." The same authority defines sexism as "assigning people specific roles in society based on gender."[2] Historically, women have been the almost exclusive objects of gender discrimination and sexism in the United States and around the world.

Some people feel that because of the physical differences between men and women, the two must be considered unequal. These people think that because only women can bear children, for example, they must be protected by special laws that apply just to them. Some of these people may also point to the animal kingdom, where males and females often have different roles. These same people point to our own past history, in which laws were often written that applied only to men, or even more specifically to white men.[3]

Over the years, however, most of these specific laws have been changed so that they apply to all people, regardless of gender. In 1920 the Nineteenth Amendment to the U.S. Constitution gave women the vote in national elections for the first time. Title VII of the 1964 Civil Rights Act gave women the same protections in employment, housing, and public accommodations that it gave blacks.[4]

In the 1970s, many women's groups organized to promote the Equal Rights Amendment (ERA). The ERA would have prohibited any discrimination based on gender. The amendment failed to win approval by the required two-thirds of all state legislatures within the necessary time limits. The debate, however, made more people aware of gender discrimination.

Countering Stereotypes of Women

Americans are more aware of women's rights than they used to be, but stereotypes of women are often still found in society. In fact, some studies show that children as young as three and four begin to act according to the gender norms, or standards for their group, that they are already beginning to learn.[5]

We can begin to combat gender stereotypes in our own lives by first discussing them. A good place to start is the mass media, which play an important role in putting forth and perpetuating stereotyped images of gender. For example, some pop music lyrics and videos, especially rap songs, have been criticized as offensive to women.

Rev. Calvin O. Butts, 3rd, an African-American minister in Harlem, has made a special crusade against hard-core rap. "You are constantly hearing, over and over, talk about mugging people, killing women, beating women, sexual behavior. When young people see this—14, 15, 16 years of age—they think this is acceptable behavior."

Others such as Richard Wesley, a successful African-American playwright and screenwriter, defend rap music as one aspect of rock music's generally antiestablishment emphasis as well as an effort by largely middle-class blacks who have succeeded to show that they have not forgotten their poorer roots.[6]

Still others are concerned about the unrealistically perfect stereotypes of women portrayed in television and in women's magazines. UCLA and Stanford psychologist Debbie Then did an in-depth survey of seventy-five women students at Stanford. Almost half the women said that the super-slim models in the magazines made them feel less confident about themselves. More than two-thirds said that they felt worse about their physical appearance from reading the magazines, even though standardized weight charts revealed that those surveyed were normal in weight. Those surveyed also said that they bought the magazines for the information in the articles, according to Dr. Then, not for the ads and photographs—which were usually touched up to appear perfect. Dr. Then quotes supermodel Cindy Crawford as saying "I think it's important for women to know that I don't wake up looking like this."[7]

Indeed, it is important for girls to know that neither negative stereotypes of women as passive victims nor positive images as "perfect ten" models are relevant to their self-esteem. People who try to use these images to manipulate women's feelings in order to make them feel less than worthy need to be told straight out by aware females that this tactic won't work.

How can gender discrimination directly affect you? In many ways— at school, in sports, at work, or out shopping.

Confronting Gender Discrimination in the Classroom

Carrie Eberhardt scored higher than any of the boys in her calculus class at South Lakes High School in Reston,

Virginia. Hearing that news, one of her classmates turned to a boy and said, "I can't believe you let the blonde...beat you." Carrie's response? "It's not the color of my hair that matters. I spend just as much time studying as you do."[8]

Discrimination against girls in school classrooms was documented in 1992 in a detailed report published by the American Association of University Women (AAUW). The report cited studies showing that teachers pay much less attention in class to girls than to boys. The report also found that textbooks still promote stereotypes, curricula often ignore female areas of concern and points of view, and schools do not encourage girls to pursue math and science.[9]

For example, research cited in the AAUW report indicated that boys in grades one to six called out answers eight times more often than girls. Furthermore teachers were more likely to listen to boys, even if they called out, while telling girls they should raise their hands if they wanted to speak. In science, one study found that 51 percent of boys in the third grade had used a microscope, while only 37 percent of the girls had; in 11th grade, 49 percent of the boys used an electricity meter, compared to only 17 percent of the girls.[10]

Many people have questioned these statistics; indeed, according to researchers, girls in school and women in the working world themselves often deny that discrimination is being practiced against them personally.[11] To understand these figures, one must look at the context in which they arise. In school, for example, while most teachers are women, 72 percent of all principals and 95 percent of all school superintendents are men. In the workplace, women still earn only 69 cents for every dollar earned by equally educated men. And despite improvement in the coverage of women in school materials, the AAUW study reports that the great majority of role models studied in class are still male. Also, problems that girls commonly face, such as sexism, eating disorders, and a relatively high suicide rate are virtually ignored in the curriculum.[12]

Critics of the AAUW report included the U.S. Education Department, which said the study lacked hard facts and depth. Diane S. Ravitch, an assistant secretary of education, commented that women have made great strides in recent decades. She noted that more women than men are now enrolled in college, in contrast with 1970, when men outnumbered women by 5 million to 3.5 million. She also noted that in 1989, 33 percent of all medical degrees went to women, up from 8 percent in 1970.[13]

Another critic of the same report was Chester E. Finn, Jr., a former assistant secretary of education. He noted the contradiction between the alleged classroom bias, or prejudice, against girls and the fact that more boys repeated grades and had inferior test scores in reading and writing.[14]

Others, however, note that by the time boys and girls take the SAT tests for college admission, boys usually score fifty to sixty points higher than girls. Furthermore, in the achievement tests—which measure knowledge in subject areas—boys outscored girls on eleven out of fourteen subjects.[15]

Traditionally wood and metal shop classes in schools have been aimed more toward boys than girls. That is changing slowly. The girls in this shop program are not only participating in wood shop run by Girls, Inc., they are being taught by women.

Whatever your opinion, gender discrimination is an issue in schools today.

Facing up to Bias in School Sports

Gender discrimination is a problem not only in the classroom, but also in the gymnasium and on the athletic field. For example, have you noticed in your school district, whether boys' or girls' teams receive more of the available funding and locker space? Lillian Potter, a seventeen-year-old senior at Walt Whitman High School in Bethesda, Maryland, suspected that boy athletes were favored in her school district. Potter wrote a letter to Montgomery County School Superintendent Paul L. Vance. She threatened to file a federal gender-discrimination complaint unless Vance corrected the big difference in emphasis and funding between boys' and girls' sports.[16]

Superintendent Vance responded to Potter by appointing her to a task force to investigate the situation. The task force report contained sixty-six recommendations for eliminating gender discrimination in county school athletic programs. The recommendations included:

- Not requiring girls' teams to set up their own playing areas.

- Equal funding from both county and booster clubs.

- Equal facilities.

- More emphasis on gender equality from athletic directors, coaches, principals, and teachers.

- Recognition of cheerleading as a sport so cheer-leaders would not have to spend their own funds on supplies.

- Establishment of a monitoring system to enforce these recommendations.

Potter, who had dropped her complaint upon being named to the task force, said she was "very, very pleased with the outcome" and "confident that these recommendations will be carried out."[17]

Some coaches in the Montgomery system, however, failed to see what all the fuss was about. One football coach said that complaints about gender bias in sports are "somebody making a big deal out of nothing." Referring to Title IX, the federal law that bans discrimination in federally financed education programs, the coach said that coaches in his school "have tripped themselves backwards to comply."[18]

Gender Discrimination in the Workplace

When women graduate from school and go into the workplace, as the great majority do today, they may also meet with gender discrimination. Since the mid-1960s, the United States Supreme Court has ruled that men and women must be treated equally in the workplace. In 1993 Ruth Bader Ginsburg, whom you read about in Chapter 1, joined the United States Supreme Court as the second woman Justice in its history. Less than a month later, the Court issued a 9-0 decision in *Harris* v. *Forklift Systems, Inc.* that made sexual harassment at work easier to prove. Sexual harassment, as defined in the *Harris* case, is a form of gender discrimination in which a person's biased behavior is so persistent that it creates a hostile or abusive work environment.[19]

Teresa Harris worked as a manager at Forklift Systems, an equipment rental company. Her boss, Charles Hardy, often insulted her because of her gender. For example, he told Harris, with other employees present, "You're a woman, what do you know?" and "We need a man as a manager." He occasionally asked Harris and other female employees to get coins from his front pants pocket. He also would throw objects on the ground and ask women workers to pick them up. After two years on the job, Harris complained to Hardy, who said he was only joking. Hardy apologized and promised to stop the offending behavior. Nevertheless the incidents continued. Harris finally quit her job and sued the company.

Previously, plaintiffs—or complaining parties—in workplace gender discrimination cases had to prove that they suffered "severe psychological injury" in order to win their case. A lower court had ruled that Harris did not suffer psychologically from her job experience. Then her case was appealed to the United States Supreme Court. There, Justice Sandra Day O'Connor, writing for the whole Court, disagreed with the lower court. O'Connor stated that the Court should look at all the factors involved in each case, not just the psychological effect on the plaintiff. Only then could the Court determine whether a hostile or abusive work environment existed. Such factors would include:

- How often the discriminatory conduct occurred.

- Whether it was physically threatening or just offensive words.

- Whether it interfered unreasonably with the person's work performance.

Gender discrimination in the workplace is an almost completely new area for the United States Supreme Court. In a 1986 opinion, *Meritor Savings Bank* v. *Vinson*, the high Court ruled that sexual harassment should be considered gender discrimination when it is so widespread that it creates a hostile or abusive work environment. However, this ruling was more general than the *Forklift* decision in 1993.[20]

Fighting Discrimination Where You Shop

Gender discrimination is against federal law in employment, housing, education, and public accommodations. But did you know that there is no federal law that prevents retail businesses and services from discriminating based on gender?

That's right. Unless there is a specific law against it in your community, city, or state, a store may legally charge a female more than a male for basically the same goods or service. The businesses most often cited as offenders of gender discrimination are auto dealerships, hair salons, and laundry and dry cleaning services.

Being Clipped or Taken to the Cleaners

A 1993 survey of one hundred hair salons and barbershops in the United States by *Money* magazine found that women usually pay from 20 to 40 percent more than men pay at the same haircutting shops—even when they have short hair.[21] A similar study of eighty haircutters in New York City conducted by the Department of Consumer Affairs the same year found that two-thirds of the shops charged women more than men. John Jay, president of a trade association for hair salon owners, explained the difference by noting that it's a carryover "from a time when ladies got hairdos, not haircuts."

In the same survey, the New York City Department of Consumer Affairs contacted eighty local dry cleaners and launderers. It discovered that women pay up to three times as much as men for exactly the same service. In addition, almost half of the study's fifty-six cleaners actually refused to launder the woman's shirt. They insisted that the shirt be dry-cleaned, at a greater cost.

Representatives of the cleaning industry explained the price difference by saying that the machine used to press shirts was designed for men's sizes. Since smaller shirts must be pressed by hand, the service costs more.[22]

If your community or city's laws do not cover gender discrimination at the hair salon or the local laundry, *Mademoiselle* magazine has some suggestions for changing the situation:

Remember—there is power in your pocketbook!

1. You can try to bargain for a lower price for a haircut, especially if you have short hair.
2. Ask to see the manager of the store in question. If you're not satisfied with the manager's response, create a pamphlet to distribute or organize a boycott of the store.
3. Take your protest to a local television station or newspaper, or even file a complaint with the local consumer affairs department or state attorney general's office.[23]

Being female in our society shouldn't be a handicap. And much of the time it no longer is—mainly because of the progress brought about by the women's movement. Nevertheless, because of a history of discrimination against females and a lingering prejudice on the part of particular people, businesses, and institutions, there is still work to be done. Remembering the examples described in this chapter may help the next time you feel discriminated against simply because of your gender.

Discrimination
Against Homosexuals

As a child, Margarethe Cammermeyer fled the Nazis when they invaded her native Norway. After arriving in the United States, she joined the Army as a nurse in 1961. She served fifteen months in Vietnam, running a hospital for wounded and dying soldiers, and was awarded the Bronze Star. She continued her Army career, and rose to the rank of colonel. In 1985 she was chosen from among 34,000 candidates across the nation as Veteran's Administration Nurse of the Year.

Despite her achievements, however, Colonel Cammermeyer was dismissed from the Army in 1992. The reason? She had been reviewed for top-secret security clearance when she applied to the Army War College. As part of the review she was asked her sexual orientation. She told the interviewer that she was a lesbian. A lesbian, or female homosexual, is a woman who is sexually attracted to other women. Solely because she was a lesbian, the Army discharged her.

Colonel Cammermeyer sued the Army, and a federal judge ruled in her favor. Under the Army policy then in force, anyone who admitted he or she was homosexual, or who was discovered to be homosexual, could be discharged from the armed services. The Army policy assumed that a homosexual orientation meant that the person intended to engage in homosexual conduct while on duty. The judge ruled, however, that there was no "rational basis" for that assumption. Cammermeyer must be returned to the Army in her old rank, said the judge, and all references to her sexual orientation erased from her record.

Since Cammermeyer's discharge, the Army has slightly changed its policy. Now those in the armed forces, and those applying to join, cannot be asked about their sexual orientation. If someone reveals that he or she is homosexual, however, that person can still be discharged. Why? Because under the new government policies, the military still assumes that a homosexual orientation means that the person intends to engage in homosexual conduct while on duty. Whether that assumption will survive other court tests to come remains to be seen.[1]

Who is homosexual? How should I act toward this person? Am I gay or lesbian? If so, how should I deal with it? These questions probably concern teenagers more than they do adults. Teenagers are at an age when their own sexuality is becoming more important to them. Homosexuality is just one aspect of this concern.

Society does not always provide much help to young people

who are coming to terms with the issue of homosexuality. In fact, the attitudes of adults toward homosexuals vary as much as the attitudes of teenagers.

On one side of the issue are those people who think of gays and lesbians only in terms of stereotypes. Some of these people may consider homosexuality a psychological problem or an illness that needs to be cured. Others in this group may believe that homosexuality is a sin that violates their religious beliefs.

Taking the opposite position are those people who accept current scientific thinking that homosexuality is determined before birth and cannot be changed. These people recognize that homosexuals do not all fit one pattern, but like heterosexuals, have a variety of lifestyles. There are also people who haven't yet made up their minds about what they believe on the issue of homosexuality.

Homosexuality has been around as long as humankind, and it is not simply going to disappear. The more informed you are, the more comfortable you are likely to feel about not only your own sexual behavior, but that of others.

Homosexuality: The Basic Facts

As we learned in Chapter 2, gays and lesbians together make up 10 percent of the population. This figure comes from the Kinsey Report on sexual practices in the United States. There are homosexuals throughout the world, not just in developed countries such as the United States. Furthermore, homosexuals have lived at all times and places in history. The following nineteenth-and twentieth-century Americans, all of whom have been described as gay, lesbian, or bisexual (attracted to both sexes), have made great contributions to our society:

James Baldwin (writer)	Martina Navratilova (athlete)
Willa Cather (writer)	Gertrude Stein (writer)
Rock Hudson (actor)	Andy Warhol (painter)
Langston Hughes (poet)	Walt Whitman (poet)
Janis Joplin (singer)	Tennessee Williams (writer)[2]

During most periods of history, gays and lesbians as a minority, have been persecuted for their sexual orientation. But they have had one advantage not available to most other groups against whom discrimination has been practiced. That advantage is "invisibility." Homosexuality can be hidden, and that fact has made it easier, in some ways, for gays to avoid confrontations with potential persecutors. In contrast, racial differences are usually noticeable. So are the marks of age, gender, and physical disability.

But "invisibility" for gays and lesbians has been a two-edged sword. While allowing some gays at least a small measure of peaceful existence, it has kept many other gays "in the closet," reluctant to reveal some of their deepest feelings or to stand up for their rights. The "invisibility" of most homosexuals has also allowed many myths and false stereotypes about gays to grow.

This gay and lesbian march on Washington, D.C. in 1993 is symbolized by two men holding hands in a show of strength, as police protect marchers from anti-gay protesters, whose posters are seen in background.

It's not true, for example, that most gay men are weak or act in a feminine way. Neither is it true that most lesbian women wear men's clothing or act in a masculine way. While some homosexuals will fit these stereotypes, so do some heterosexuals. Most homosexuals are also like heterosexuals in that they establish long-term sexual relationships. Others, again like some heterosexuals, may change partners once or more. And some gays or lesbians may even get married to partners of the opposite sex, usually to avoid being identified as homosexuals.

Not surprisingly, however, most homosexuals want to be accepted as they are and as full members of society. To expand people's concept of who gays and lesbians are and to further their acceptance, Deb Price, who is a lesbian, writes a weekly column on homosexual issues. The column appears in more than three dozen newspapers across the nation. Price doesn't see the column so much as a political platform, but rather as a way to sketch a more fully rounded portrait of gays and lesbians: churchgoing gays, lesbians facing breast cancer, or a gay gardening club as well as her own domestic life with a female spouse. "My mission is to get homosexuality away from controversy and have people see it as commonplace."[3]

Fighting Anti-Gay Discrimination

Price's mission has a long history. During the 1940s and 1950s in the United States, homosexuality was considered at best a disease, and at worst, a crime. When the Kinsey Report was published in 1948, Alfred Kinsey, a biologist, found that about 13 percent of adult American males and about 7 percent of females—or an average of one out of every ten Americans—were homosexual. Americans were shocked. Many denied or tried to suppress the evidence in the report. Still, the basic conclusion—that homosexuality is a fixed sexual orientation—has been later confirmed by other studies.[4] The American Psychiatric Association struck homosexuality from its list of mental disorders in 1973.[5]

During the sexual revolution of the 1960s, gays and lesbians became more of a community with common interests. Large numbers of gays and lesbians were now living in distinct neighborhoods in cities such as San Francisco and New York.

On June 27, 1969, an event occurred that, by all accounts, for the first time inspired gay communities across the country to become a political force. Police in New York City's Greenwich Village, where many homosexuals lived, made a routine raid of a gay bar called the Stonewall Inn. Instead of following police orders, however, the bar's gay patrons and sympathetic neighborhood residents fought back. News of their resistance swept the country. Symbolically at least, the gay liberation movement was born. The day is now celebrated in many cities around the world as part of an annual Gay Pride Week.[6]

Perhaps the biggest challenge to the gay rights movement since the 1980s has been the epidemic of the HIV infection and AIDS. AIDS can be contracted and spread by anyone. But in the United States and Canada it appeared at first mainly among male homosexuals. In 1993 about 47 percent of the 103,500 reported new AIDS cases resulted from male-to-male sexual contact, down from 67 percent in 1985. During the same eight-year period, however, AIDS cases among heterosexuals increased from about 2 percent to almost 9 percent of the total number of cases.[7]

The fight to increase research on the HIV virus and AIDS, in order to more effectively treat the disease, has been waged mainly by the gay and lesbian community. Because the HIV virus and AIDS are identified with gays and lesbians, many members of these communities fear that they will feel more discrimination as a result.

Organizing and Suing for Gay Rights

Protests such as the Stonewall uprising dramatically signaled the gay and lesbian movement's growing power. Most of the muscle in the movement, however, has come from the less exciting process of political organizing and challenging existing laws in court. An increasing number of large corporations such as Levi Strauss, Apple, and Lotus provide at least some benefits to the partners of their homosexual employees.[8] By 1992, 21 states and 130 cities (including 31 of the 50 largest cities) had laws that provided at least some legal protection against anti-gay discrimination. We may, thus, conclude that "almost half the people in the United States now either live in states or cities that have such laws or work in jobs where nondiscrimination is mandated [required] by administrative regulations, civil-service rules, union contracts, or other enforceable policies."[9]

These victories, while significant in themselves, have not reached a point where public opinion has moved decisively in favor of gay rights. Almost half the states still have laws discriminating against homosexuals, though they are rarely enforced. In 1986 the United States Supreme Court ruled 5-4 in the case of *Bowers* v. *Hardwick* that the prosecution of a gay couple for homosexual acts in their own bedroom was not a violation of federal privacy laws.[10] This was certainly a defeat in the battle to gain rights for homosexuals.

The results of a *Newsweek* poll taken right before the 1992 presidential election revealed significant differences in opinion about different aspects of homosexuality among Americans.

Is homosexuality an acceptable alternative lifestyle?
41%–*Yes*   53%–*No*

Should homosexuals have equal rights in job opportunities?
78%–*Yes*   17%–*No*

In other words, most Americans overwhelmingly support equal employment rights for gays and lesbians, but are not so sure they approve of gay and lesbian behavior in general.[11]

This ambivalence has expressed itself during the 1990s in an increase in violent incidents and the passage of local laws against gay rights. In general, however, courts have supported laws that ban discrimination against gays and lesbians in housing and employment.

Fighting Discrimination Against Homosexuals in the Schools

Though most homosexuals sense at an early age, that they are "different" most recognize their homosexuality between fourteen and sixteen years for males and between sixteen and nineteen years for females. For this reason schools are an especially important place in which homosexuality is often confronted.[12]

We have seen society's confused attitude about homosexuality in general. Since our schools reflect society, it is not surprising that schools are doing only a fair-to-poor job of dealing with the issues surrounding homosexuality. Research shows that 45 percent of gay men and 20 percent of lesbian women experience verbal or physical assault in high school. As a result of this harassment, 28 percent of these students are forced to drop out of school.[13] No doubt largely because of this harassment as well, 80 percent of lesbian, gay, and bisexual youth also report feeling extremely isolated from their peers.[14]

Sensitive and comprehensive sex education courses can help lessen the ignorance and fear that result from this isolation. One study by the Center of Educational Policy Analysis found that directly dealing with often-avoided topics such as sexual orientation is the best way to reduce the risks of inappropriate teenage sexual activity. In one New Jersey school district, the sex education teacher Suzanne Westenhoefer is herself a lesbian. She finds that the best way to teach about homosexuality is to directly confront teenagers' stereotypes on the subject and answer their questions with a mixture of fact and humor. (In fact, Ms. Westenhoefer is by night a professional comic at New York City area night clubs.)[15]

Another method of dealing with discrimination against homosexuals in high school is to teach gays and lesbians in a separate facility until they have developed enough self-confidence to enable them to enter mainstream classrooms. The Harvey Milk School in New York is a joint project of the New York City Board of Education and the Hetrick-Martin Institute, a nonprofit organization that provides services to young gay people. The curriculum of the Harvey Milk School is like that of any other public high school. The goal of the school is to prepare these students to function in the wider world by providing them a nonthreatening atmosphere in which to pursue their studies. Once students gain new skills and confidence, they are encouraged to return to their original schools if possible.[16]

Civil libertarians such as Norman Siegel of the New York Civil Liberties Union have criticized the school. "If you're disturbed about the creation of separatist schools on the basis of race and sex," says Siegel, "then separatism on the basis of sexual orientation would seem to be suspect as well." Supporters of the school include Sandra Feldman of the United Federation of Teachers. While critical of the school at first, she now praises it for "turning youngsters with very special and sensitive problems back into the mainstream and doing a wonderful job with it."[17]

As the gay and lesbian rights movement has become more active and visible, it has brought more understanding from some people, while inciting others to be more openly hostile. A study released in 1991 by the National Gay and Lesbian Task Force reported an average increase of 42 percent in that year in hate crimes against gays and lesbians, including physical assaults, harassment, bomb threats, vandalism, and arson.[18]

Commenting on the study, Adele Terrell of the National Institute Against Prejudice and Violence noted that this increase is matched by increases in violence against other minority groups. She thinks the increases are caused by "economic decline, demographic [population] change, and political gains made by minority groups," which have "caused some people to look for scapegoats [persons to blame]."[19] There is no doubt that the increase in both the size and visibility of minority groups, including gays and lesbians, is upsetting to some people. But to blame minority groups for a stagnant economy and economic hardship, is really to miss the point. Gays and lesbians as well as other minorities are just as affected by economic downturns as any other group in society.

As homosexuality becomes more visible, people are finding out that, like most groups, gays and lesbians have a wide range of lifestyles and viewpoints. In the 1988 presidential election, for example, George Bush supported the Americans with Disabilities Act, which prohibits discrimination against people with HIV or AIDS. Partly as a result, Bush received at least 35 percent of the gay and lesbian vote. In the 1992 election, on the other hand, Bill Clinton openly courted gay and lesbian groups and appeared to receive more votes from these groups than Bush.[20]

Similarly, more and more gays and lesbians are now pushing for some form of legal recognition for long-term unions. This development is partly the result of AIDS. Partners of gay men who died without having written wills suddenly found that they had no legal claim on property that under the law would have gone to the dead man's spouse. The move, however, is also the result of gay couples' desire to give their children—whether they come from a previous heterosexual marriage, through adoption, through artifical insemination, or by other means—the legal rights that other children enjoy. Psychological studies overwhelmingly show no adverse effects on children from being raised by homosexual parents, though there is some feeling that studies should follow such children into adolescence in order to be valid.[21]

As more people recognize that gays and lesbians have much in common with other people, a growing majority of Americans will likely oppose discrimination against homosexuals. While there will probably be some who find it difficult to accept gays and lesbians as equal members of society, this discriminating minority will have to fight a legal system that is increasingly sympathetic to gay and lesbian rights.

6

Age Discrimination

Elizabeth Sobol, was a successful managing director for the utility-finance group in the investment-banking division of Kidder Peabody, a large Wall Street firm owned by General Electric. A new chief executive of Kidder wrote a confidential memo to top General Electric executives. The memo listed those employees he thought were Kidder's most important talent. Not one of those on the list was over the age of forty-nine. Sobol herself was told there was "too much gray hair" in her department and that she should fire several older workers. Five of the six she was told to fire were over fifty years old. This left eight people in her department, of whom Sobol was the oldest. Then, at the age of forty-seven, Sobol herself was forced out.[1]

But Sobol fought back. Responding to her efforts and those of sixteen other former Kidder workers, the federal Equal Employment Opportunities Commission (EEOC) filed the largest suit ever against a securities firm, on the grounds that Kidder practiced age discrimination.

Fighting the Myth of the "Throwaway" Older Worker

The Kidder chief held a common misperception that older workers are not as productive as younger ones. Yet the advantages of hiring older workers were confirmed in a recent study conducted by ICF Inc., a Washington, D.C. consulting firm. ICF studied older workers in three companies in the United States and Great Britain.

Days Inn, a large motel chain in the United States, found that its older workers took no more time to be trained than younger workers. They also found that older workers tended to stay on the job longer, thus saving the company over $600 per worker. While older workers were not quite as fast as younger workers, they were more successful at attracting business. Travelers Corporation, a financial services company, had similar results using retired workers and older employees to fill temporary positions. In this way, the company saved almost $1 million in 1989 with no loss in efficiency. B&Q, the largest houseware/hardware chain in Britain, staffed an entire store with workers over fifty years old. The store was 18 percent more profitable than the average of five similar B&Q stores with younger workers. Also, lost or damaged stock was much less and older workers were less likely to be absent or to quit.[2]

Too many people silently assume that younger workers are more energetic, have more creative ideas, and are generally better suited to a company that is undergoing major changes in the way it works. Yet research on older workers shows that common beliefs about the gradual wear and tear on the brain after age twenty-five are not based on basic knowledge of the brain's function. In fact, older employees can be a valuable asset if they, like other employees, are trained to adapt to changes in the company.[3] Just as the value of workers older than fifty is too often underestimated, so is the value of the majority of those over sixty-five. Most are active, mentally alert, and not that different from their younger selves. In the past, advertising and the media emphasized the attractions of being young; the public was left to assume that older people did not lead attractive lives. Today, organizations such as the Gray Panthers, which monitors media programming and advertising, are helping us get a more accurate image of older people. But there is still much work to be done.[4]

Grace Payne, in her seventies, is just one of millions of senior citizens who lead full lives. Since 1972 she has been executive director of the largest non-profit social service agency in Watts, the Los Angeles community where violence erupted after the Rodney King verdict in April 1992. Her center provides child care, a shelter for homeless women, rehabilitation for retarded adults, youth development, a credit union, and housing counseling.[5]

Do you think that getting older means hanging up your swimsuit, running shoes, or racing bicycle? Then you haven't met sixty-eight-year-old Don Greetham and the tens of thousands of senior athletes who compete every two years in the U.S. National Senior Sports Classic. Anyone over fifty-five who can pass a simple stress test can compete in this event. Greetham's training includes an hour of swimming four or five times a week. The myth that most older Americans should cut down on their exercise is just that—a myth. "I would never advocate that," says Mary E. Case, M.D., the St. Louis County medical examiner. "On balance, your health risks are much lower if you exercise."[6]

Following Up on Discrimination Against Older Workers

We have seen the talents offered by older workers and senior citizens. Yet more senior employees are being laid off than ever before, as measured by the numbers of age discrimination suits being filed.

From 1981 to 1991 the number of age discrimination lawsuits rose 24 percent, or more than 2 percent a year.[7] In the year ending September 30, 1993, the EEOC handled about 20,000 complaints, up 32 percent from the 1989 period.[8]

As a watchdog of those fired because of age, however, the EEOC has not often been very helpful. In only 1.5 percent of the complaints it received in 1990, for example, did the EEOC bring charges against the offending employer. Some people blame budget cuts for lack of EEOC effectiveness; others blame lack of political will. Usually, dismissed employees must file their own expensive and time-consuming lawsuits.

For example, Richard Rathemacher, a fifty-three-year-old systems-engineering manager with thirty years of experience at IBM, was passed over for a promotion. His boss said he wanted "new young blood" in the job. Then Rathemacher was transferred to a sales job for which he had no training. Soon after, he was told he should consider early retirement at fifty-five, because his next job evaluation was going to be unsatisfactory. To make sure Rathemacher got the message, he was then demoted and sent to an abandoned IBM branch office where he sat alone with nothing to do in a 10,000-square-foot space. Finally Rathemacher reluctantly agreed to take early retirement. He then sued IBM for age discrimination.

At the trial, IBM insisted that it did not discriminate by age. The company painted a picture of an employee who did not get along well with people and who had retired voluntarily. The jury disagreed, however, and awarded Rathemacher $315,000, plus attorney's fees. IBM appealed the verdict. In the meantime, Rathemacher, now fifty-nine, has been unable to find another job.[9]

One example of a person whom the EEOC was able to help is Mrs. Todd Ryan-Millington, seventy-eight, who was laid off from her job as sales office manager of a textile company. She filed an age discrimination complaint with the EEOC. The EEOC investigated her case and those of two other dismissed employees from the same company who were over forty. Three years later Ryan-Millington won an out-of-court settlement of $99,000 after the EEOC threatened to file a federal lawsuit. But Ryan-Millington was one of the lucky ones. Unless a dismissed employee can prove specific age discrimination, it's very difficult to win the case. Most people don't even try.[10]

Investigating Discrimination Against Children and Young Adults

Not all age discrimination is aimed at older workers and senior citizens. In Chapter 1 you read how one company discriminated against teenagers by firing them in order to avoid dealing with possible federal suits under child labor laws. Other examples of discrimination against the young, such as those that follow, have also been documented.

- A ten-year-old is not allowed to accompany his parents into an art museum.

- A thirteen-year-old is kept from visiting her mother in the hospital.

- A sixteen-year-old is barred from shopping in a downtown department store.

Many teens could offer examples of discrimination similar to these. In some towns and cities, for example, children under a certain age are routinely prevented from entering certain restaurants and clubs. Restaurants say that such children tend to be noisy and annoy other diners. Yet in Europe children suffer no such fate. In some cases, popular clubs have been well known for keeping possible patrons out for a variety of reasons, including their age.

Museums plead that their works of art are too valuable to risk damage from those too young to appreciate their worth. But are most children really unable to appreciate the value of a work of art? Hospitals claim that keeping out children aged thirteen and under is done to protect patients and staff, since children usually carry a higher number of contagious diseases than older age groups. But what about the mental health of the patient who is prevented from seeing his or her young child, and that of the child who is forbidden to see his or her ill parent? In each case, a rule intended to prevent problems may end up affecting many "innocent" people.

Of course, sometimes there are valid reasons for age-based rules. Hardly any adult would argue against the law that, in most states, forbids the sale of alcoholic beverages to those under twenty-one. Nor would most adults argue against the system of rating movies as *G, PG, PG-13,* and *R.* But other age-specific rules have come under increasing attack. In 1993, for example, New York City passed a law ruling that children, teenagers, or senior citizens cannot be kept from public places and public services because of their age. The rule would seem to apply to most, if not all, of the preceding examples.[11]

Some observers, however, wonder whether such laws might force businesses to give up their efforts to attract a specific kind of audience. Might some restaurants that require a coat and tie for men, for example, be forced to give up that rule because it is discriminatory? And what about the movie chain that, with patron approval, doesn't permit children under six to attend a movie after 6 P.M. unless that movie is aimed at a family audience?

Obviously the issue of age discrimination can rather quickly expand to include the debate of individual or group rights versus the rights of the whole state or society.

Finding Common Ground Among Different Age Groups in Society

So far in this chapter we've discussed discrimination against the young and the old separately, as if the interests of these two groups are quite different. For example, the elderly as a group have been accused of collecting more than their fair share of Social Security benefits. At the same time, younger workers have seen their Social Security payments sharply increase, partly to pay for these benefits.[12]

In reality, Social Security helps not only retired workers, but also over three million children whose parents are retired, disabled, or deceased. In fact, almost four million children live in households where someone receives Social Security.[13] (This issue will be discussed in more detail in Chapter 8.)

But think about this question: Are the goals of the young and the old really that different? Both groups certainly want to be accepted by others for who they are. Both groups simply ask for an equal place in society—a seat at the dining room table, so to speak, not sole rights to the whole house.

In previous generations, the typical family—a married

Despite widely different backgrounds, bonds between young and old can and do develop, if given the opportunity. Each group can fill the unfulfilled needs of the other. The students in this picture are sharing a story with the members of a Senior Center.

couple, only one of whom worked, children, and grandparents nearby—may have provided the necessary bonds between old and young. Today, however, only 9 percent of American households fit that family model. The links between old and young must, thus, be formed in new ways.

Two programs suggest some of the many ways in which old and young may be brought together to help each other and to help do away with stereotypes. In the first program, senior citizens at a Senior Center were visited by students from a nearby middle school as part of a textbook unit on immigration. The students interviewed the senior citizens, many of whom had been immigrants themselves, to find out what sort of experiences they had had when they first came to the United States. With their positive outlook on life, despite its hardships, these senior citizens provided a valuable resource for students, who often had their own worries about their own future.[14]

The second program, Foster Grandparents, is actually a group of programs involving senior citizens and youth who might otherwise be out on the street and in danger of causing trouble. In one Foster Grandparents program, retired workers and older volunteers provided role models for teenage mothers. In another program older people worked with youthful offenders. In a third program, older adult role models worked with students who were in danger of dropping out of school.

In each case, despite widely different backgrounds, bonds between old and young did develop. Some of these links were so strong that they resembled those of actual family members;

other bonds were more like those between friendly neighbors. All youth in the program appeared to benefit, even those that did not form any particular bond. The older adults benefited as well: They were able to pass on some of the wisdom that comes with age and they were able to meet the important challenge of helping youth change their lives.

Why did the unusual combination of youth and age work? Observers note that the two groups bonded because they met each other's needs. The youth were "lonely, at a time of crisis, ready for change and desirous of adult contact," while many of the elders were "enthusiastic but also lonely and intent on finding meaningful roles in their senior years."[15]

Observers noted that these programs were successful for the elders for three other reasons. First, the elders were given complete freedom in meeting with the young people. Second, it was made clear to the elders from the beginning that their purpose in working with these youths was to perform any task—for example tutoring—not as an end in itself, but as a way of building trust and friendship. Third, the seniors received support from their sponsoring organizations in handling problems that occurred.[16]

What lesson do these examples of intergenerational cooperation hold for American society as a whole? Perhaps the lesson can be stated as follows. All citizens of our country are, in an important sense, members of one community. As in any true community, in our country we are all in some way responsible for the welfare of others. When there are floods in the Midwest, for example, citizens from the whole nation pitch in with their muscle and tax dollars to help. People help others not just because they know that under our democratic government citizens of the Midwest would do the same for them. People help their fellow citizens simply because that is what being a citizen of a community means. In the same way, young and old help each other because they, too, are both citizens of the same community or nation. Only when people in a community work for the common good, as well as for their own advantage, will discrimination of any kind cease to be a problem.

7

Discrimination Against People With Disabilities

It was a beautiful summer day. Marilyn Hamilton's colorful hang glider soared over a California valley, floating along with the rising air currents. Then the air currents suddenly gave out. Hamilton's hang glider crashed nose-down into the side of a mountain. Her spinal cord was bruised by the impact, making her a paraplegic. She could not move or feel anything from the waist down. Hamilton now had a physical disability.[1]

According to the Americans with Disabilities Act (ADA) of 1990, a person with a disability is someone who may now have, or has had in the past, a physical or mental injury or condition that greatly limits one or more major life activities. Such activities include moving, seeing, hearing, speaking, or thinking. Under the ADA, even if you don't actually have a disability but are considered by others to have one, then you are considered to be a person with a disability. The ADA prohibits discrimination against people with physical or mental disabilities in employment, transportation, public accommodations, and telecommunications.[2]

There are perhaps forty-three million persons with varying degrees of disability in the United States. Almost all of them have been discriminated against—often by people who aren't even aware of their prejudice. Why?

People discriminate against those with disabilities partly out of ignorance. Most people without disabilities simply don't know very much about having a disability. They may not personally know, or think they know, anyone who has a disability. So when facing a person with a disability, they may have incorrect beliefs.

In fact, people with disabilities are really not much different in their needs and wants than people without disabilities. As one writer points out, like other workers, people with disabilities want to show what they can accomplish. "They want performance appraisals [judgments] based on facts, not assumptions [beliefs]. And they want control of their environment to the greatest extent possible. This includes being independent and being able to influence activities around them."[3]

People may also discriminate against those with disabilities out of fear. Some fear a person with a disability, because they are not sure what is appropriate or helpful behavior in the presence of such a person. If the fear of disability is too strong for a person without a disability to handle, he or she may try to get rid of the feeling by projecting it onto the person who triggered that fear. This displaced fear can take the form of anger toward the person with the disability, depression, or even denial that a disability exists.

Once Marilyn recovered enough from her hang gliding accident to operate a wheelchair, she noticed that people acted differently toward her. "I knew I was the same as always," she says. "I just got around by a different means of transportation."[4] Yet her doctor sometimes talked to Marilyn's husband as if Marilyn wasn't present. Sometimes friends seemed so depressed looking at her that Marilyn felt she had to be the one to cheer them up rather than vice versa.

In some ways, Marilyn was lucky. She had an uncle who was a quadriplegic, a person who has lost the use of both arms and both legs. Marilyn's uncle became an important role model for her. Marilyn also had two hang-gliding friends who helped her design and build a lightweight wheelchair so that she could get around more quickly and play sports such as tennis. In time, Marilyn's lightweight wheelchair became so well known that she and her two friends formed a successful wheelchair manufacturing company that grew to have sales of $40 million a year. Her product is now imitated by other wheelchair companies.[5]

Marilyn had energy, ambition, and role models. But what about those people with disabilities who may require more guidance and support?

Mainstreaming Students with Disabilities in Schools: Pro and Con

In 1970, according to the U.S. Census, 750,000 children between the ages of seven and thirteen did not attend school.

The student on the left cannot see. She is getting help with her school work from her teacher and a device called the Kurzweil vocal scanner. It scans the words on a printed page and vocalizes them. The student can control the speed of the reading and even choose among different voices for the "reader."

Marian Wright Edelman, founder of the Children's Defense Fund, was surprised by this number and decided to investigate. She found that these children were not minority children, as she had suspected. They were children with disabilities whom the schools had rejected. The group included those who were retarded or autistic as well as those with cerebral palsy, muscular dystrophy, spina bifida, or paralysis. School officials said they did not have the resources to educate these children. Edelman, however, did not accept that argument. She helped the parents of these neglected children to organize and press for an equal education for people with disabilities.[6]

The result of the parents' campaign was a new federal law, the Education for All Handicapped Children Act of 1975. This law guarantees a free and appropriate education for all of the nation's children with disabilities between the ages of three and twenty-one. The law further states that, whenever possible, this education is to take place with children who have no disability. The United States Supreme Court has affirmed the right of even the child with the most severe disability to have an education. In practice, however, grouping students with disabilities with other students, or "mainstreaming," has usually meant putting students with disabilities into the same building as children without disabilities, but not into the same classroom. More recently, however, parents have been demanding that the education of students with disabilities be truly integrated.[7] These parents might cite the example of *Brown* v. *Board of Education* as support. Whether talking of students with disabilities or students of different racial and ethnic backgrounds, these parents say, a separate education is unequal by definition.

Many parents and researchers have concluded that integrating students with disabilities into nondisabled classes provides an education superior to that provided by "segregated" classes. In Johnson City, New York, about 185 of its 200 special education students are now taught in regular classrooms. Test scores have risen in the first three years of the program for both regular students and students with disabilities who have been mainstreamed. Students without disabilities received special training before they joined students with disabilities in the classroom. Friendships have been formed between members of the two groups. Yet advocates for people with disabilities worry that such mainstreaming will cause funding for separate services to students with disabilities to be cut by schools under financial pressure—even though such funding is required by law.[8]

Critics of mainstreaming also charge that the practice only works in small districts that have both a reputation for new ideas and specially trained teachers to help students with disabilities. Critics also cite a long-range study showing that 61 percent of students with learning disabilities eventually fail at least one course when they are placed in a regular class. Only 14 percent of such students fail who remain in special education classes.[9]

After years of isolation, young students with disabilities face many challenges, whether or not they enter the educational mainstream. Yet these students will also have increasing numbers of role models. The first generation of students with disabilities to grow up under the full protection of the Education for All Handicapped Children Act began graduating from college in the early 1990s.[10]

Fighting Job Discrimination Against People With Disabilities

Not too long ago it was assumed that the great majority of people with disabilities would never have a normal life that included marriage, job, and family. This stereotype has long since been proven incorrect. However, many people with disabilities are still unemployed and suffer from discrimination in the job market.[11]

Charles Wessel was the head of a private detective agency in Chicago when he was diagnosed with inoperable brain cancer. After missing a number of days of work, he was dismissed. Wessel sued the company, arguing that he still could do his job when he was fired. He won $572,000 when his company was found guilty in the first case of employment discrimination under the ADA.[12]

Under the ADA, which went into effect in 1992, no employer can discriminate against someone because of a disability if the individual is otherwise qualified for a job. The law applies to job applications, hiring and firing of workers, salaries, promotions, job training, and other aspects of employment.[13] The law also requires that businesses eliminate structural barriers that prevent any person with a disability from using any facility open to the public.[14]

Businesses have found it relatively easy to meet the ADA's requirements for physical changes such as accessible bathrooms, ramps, and raised tables. Employers have trouble, however, dealing with less definable issues such as back problems or mental illness. Discrimination based on these two complaints together accounted for almost a third of cases brought during the first year under the ADA.[15]

For example, autism is a mental condition, affecting about 200,000 Americans, in which the individual is apparently unable to communicate with others, or in many cases even to speak. About 70 percent of all autistic people have some degree of mental retardation. An additional 10 percent, though retarded, have amazing gifts in some areas such as music or mathematics. A recent fictional example, based on a real person, was Raymond Babbitt, played by Dustin Hoffman in the Academy-award-winning film *Rain Man.* Like Raymond, autistic persons for many years were kept in institutions or otherwise isolated and thought to be "hopeless." Today, however, it has been shown that autistics can be helped; and about 300,000 have even become productive workers.[16]

One success story involves Charles Novotny, who works putting together fuses for nuclear submarines for FIC Corporation. It turns out that some autistics have a fascination with mechanical objects, and are very good at tasks that require repetition and precision. Novotny was helped by a special job coach who is trained to work with autistics and who is paid by a nonprofit group based in Rockville, Maryland, called Community Services for Autistic Adults and Children (CSAAC). With his CSAAC coach's help, Novotny became a highly effective worker. Novotny's job involves twisting thin metal threads around a small resistor. Through employment, autistics such as Novotny and his work partner, Mary Sauerbier, have become more sociable; at the same time, their nondisabled colleagues have developed new respect for people with disabilities.[17]

Employers may well ask, however, if there shouldn't be some reasonable limit to what they must pay to accommodate the worker with a disability. For example, if a company must spend $5,000 to accommodate a person's particular disability, is the worker still an economic advantage to the company? Probably he or she is, if that cost is weighed against the Workers' Compensation that the company would have to pay the worker for doing nothing. At IFC Corporation, there is no doubt that the autistic workers' productivity is worth more than any extra money that is spent in training or supervising the autistic workers. In some jobs, Novotny and Sauerbier now perform up to 200 percent better than their coworkers with no disabilities.[18]

Corporations Confront Myths and Realities About Workers With Disabilities

We read in Chapter 6 that elderly workers, contrary to myth, are usually as valuable, or even more valuable, than other workers. The same is true of workers with disabilities, according to studies quoted by Carolyn Wiley. The studies destroy several myths about hiring people with a disability, including the following:

Myth: Workers with disabilities are absent more and leave the company sooner.

Reality: According to the U.S. Office of Vocational Rehabilitation, workers with disabilities have no more absences and turnover than fully abled people.

Myth: Workers with disabilities produce less.

Reality: Workers with disabilities generally appreciate more the chance to work, and therefore, tend to be more conscientious and to produce more than abled employees.

Myth: Workers with disabilities pose a greater safety risk.

Reality: According to the U.S. Office of Vocational Rehabilitation, "90 percent of employees with disabilities have the same records of accidents as other workers, and only 2 percent have worse records."

Myth: Employees with disabilities are costly to the company.

Reality: A company must be accessible to customers with disabilities as well as to their employees with disabilities. Sixty percent of the changes required to allow workers with disabilities to perform their jobs "cost less than $100, and 90 percent cost less than $1,000. The average cost is $50."[19]

Several corporations and institutions have taken steps in their employment programs to correct these myths. Marriott Corporation, the nationwide hotel chain, decided to hire people with mental and physical disabilities to help solve industry-wide problems of high turnover and fewer workers. Marriott took advantage of federal tax incentives that not only benefit the company, but also save taxpayers from $5,000 to $10,000 per worker per year. This money would otherwise go to support an unemployed worker with a disability.[20]

In eleven years, McDonald's restaurants have trained 9,000 workers with disabilities to work in forty-seven restaurants in twenty-two states under the McJobs program. The workers' disabilities range from minor to severe, including those with visual, hearing, or orthopedic impairments as well as mental retardation and learning disabilities. Almost 90 percent of those trained end up as McDonald's employees. The program is partially funded by individual states at a rate of $800 per trainee.[21]

Helping People with Disabilities Achieve Their Full Potential

As we have seen, under the ADA people with disabilities have won the right to their fair share in the land of opportunity. That victory, however, is only half the battle. Now we must educate everyone else in how to accommodate their colleagues with disabilities. The ignorant or fearful people who did not know how to treat Marilyn Hamilton in her wheelchair can still be found. How do we reach those who discriminate, some without even realizing what they are doing?

Perhaps the best way to help the nondisabled feel what it is like to have a disability is through simulations. Simulations are role-playing exercises in which the people with no disabilities "acquire" disabilities. At Meridian Bancorp Inc., for example, a teller who is not disabled plays the role of a customer in a wheelchair who must deal with the fact that teller window is too high. In other exercises, employees smear petroleum jelly on a pair of eyeglasses and try to read something through them, listen to audiotapes while wearing earplugs, and try to write checks while their fingers are taped together.

In simulating degrees of deafness, blindness, and paralysis, employees without disabilities gain a new understanding and respect for what people with disabilities face in everyday life. These employees also begin to understand how much more people with disabilities can achieve with some very basic changes on the employer's part in promoting physical accommodation and better understanding.[22]

Christopher Bell, a former EEOC lawyer who helped write the ADA, describes the problem of how the employer without a disability may perceive the employee who has a disability: "For years, being fair meant treating everyone the same. Employers are uncomfortable with accommodations [for those with a disability] because that's treating someone differently."[23]

Yet in a sense employers have already made accommodations

to their workers without disabilities by giving them special training, designing their offices and equipment to assure maximum output, and so on. Those employees with a disability now simply require a different kind of accommodation in order to assure them they can work at the maximum level that their talents allow.

8

The Future
of Discrimination

As we look back over the various kinds of discrimination examined in this book, we can see in each case signs of progress as well as continuing problems. This mixed pattern makes it difficult to predict the future with any certainty.

Mixed Results of the Fight Against Racial Discrimination

Because of the achievements of the civil rights movement of the 1960s, African Americans now fill elected offices across the nation in record numbers. African Americans graduate from high school and college at an all-time high rate. A sizable African-American middle class has arisen with new political and economic power. Yet the situation that sparked the first United States Supreme Court decision to deal with inequality—school segregation—has proved more difficult to change.

True, there are no longer legally separate public schools for blacks and whites, as there were before *Brown* v. *Board of Education.* Still, a 1993 study by the National School Boards Association (NSBA) shows that 66 percent of African-American children in the United States attend schools with mostly minority students. As few as 39 percent of African-American students attended all-black schools from 1968 to 1972, during the height of court-ordered busing. Since then, however, three factors have combined to virtually resegregate many urban school systems: (1) population trends; (2) more conservative court decisions on busing as a way of ending segregation; and (3) continuing segregation in housing.[1]

These same factors have also affected the growing Hispanic population in the United States. In fact, Hispanic Americans, not African Americans, are now the most segregated students in the nation's public schools. The NSBA study notes that 74 to 78 percent of all Hispanic-American students attend schools with mostly minority students.[2]

Of the three factors that have led to lack of progress in desegregation, segregated housing is probably the most important. According to two experts in the field, "Until the black ghetto is [taken to pieces] as a basic institution of American urban life, progress in [decreasing] racial inequality in other arenas will be slow, fitful, and incomplete."[3]

It would be wrong, however, to emphasize only the problems in overcoming racial discrimination. When viewed in retrospect, there has been notable progress in overcoming many aspects of racial discrimination over the last forty years. In addition to the advances in African-American educational achievement and economic status already noted, we should also examine the increasing recognition by traditionally white institutions of other advantages of diversity in American society. In corporations, for example, "diversity breeds new ideas, styles, and new methods in solving problems," according to one manager at Unisys Corporation.[4]

A report by the Hudson Institute, a research organization, estimates that 85 percent of all new entrants to the United States workforce will soon be women, minorities, and immigrants; only 15 percent of new entrants will be native white males. Since corporations have a big investment in their employees, for these organizations diversity will now become a bottom-line issue. If corporations are to attract, train, and retain their employees, the companies must learn how to manage cultural diversity. This economic motive should make it more likely that these companies will be successful. And their success can only benefit American society as a whole.[5]

The Seesaw Battle to End Gender Discrimination

It sometimes seems that for every victory in the fight against gender discrimination, there is a defeat, even though gradual progress continues. We have seen how the United States Supreme Court ruled 9-0 in *Harris* v. *Forklift Systems* that women no longer needed to show psychological harm in

93

order to prove that they were sexually harassed in the workplace. Yet within months, newspapers began citing reports that many companies were now requiring all new employees as well as those up for promotions to sign agreements in which they gave up any right to sue their company as a condition of employment.[6]

Under these agreements, any differences between employee and employer would be settled by binding arbitration. In binding arbitration, judges selected by both employer and employee decide which side is correct, and both parties agree to abide by the decision. While the costs of such an agreement are less for both sides than going to court, the disadvantage for the employee is that any monetary damages are usually much less. In addition, there are two advantages for the employer in binding arbitration: (1) the employer has more control over the proceedings by being able to veto any selection of judges who had proved unsympathetic in the past; (2) all testimony is confidential, so the employer has more control over its public image.[7]

Many companies are waiting to see how Congress and the United States Supreme Court deal with the issue of gender discrimination in the workplace before they put similar policies in place.

You have already read in Chapter 4 how gender discrimination in the classroom, in sports, and in consumer affairs as well as in the workplace has provided continuing examples of disagreement over the basic issue of gender equality. Recently, however, the Supreme Court of the United States has been issuing generally supportive opinions in cases of gender discrimination. It therefore seems likely that the message of gender equality will gradually get across to the whole society.

In one key case in 1992 the United States Supreme Court ruled 9-0 in *Franklin* v. *Gwinnett County Public Schools* that students may now sue for monetary damages in gender discrimination cases. A high school student named Christine Franklin said that a teacher had pursued her for more than a year and forced her to have sexual relations. School officials took no action. Although they were aware of the problem, they discouraged the student from pressing criminal charges. When the teacher resigned, the school closed its investigation. Now that their pocketbooks may be affected, however, educational institutions, like corporations, may be much less likely to try to shrug off potential gender discrimination problems.[8]

Gay and Lesbian Rights Movement Gains, But Not Steadily

We noted in Chapter 5 that the gay and lesbian rights movement has seen both victories and defeats in recent years, reflecting mixed public opinion on the subject. Perhaps no area better illustrates the conflicting attitudes of Americans toward homosexuality than the debate over gays and lesbians in the military. While homosexuals have always served in the military, of course, until recently they had served in secrecy. If they revealed their homosexuality, they were thrown out of the service.

In 1992 presidential candidate Bill Clinton proposed

to allow homosexuals to serve openly in the military. As President, however, Clinton backed down when his proposal was challenged. Instead he agreed to a compromise with the Joint Chiefs of Staff. Under this plan potential enlistees would not be asked if they were homosexual.

Once they were members of the military, however, they would be required not to reveal their homosexuality. This plan, often summarized as "don't ask, don't tell," was widely criticized by liberals and the gay and lesbian community as another example of discrimination against homosexuals as a group.

One encouraging note for the future of homosexuality in the United States was heard in March 1994. For the first time, the United States Immigration and Naturalization Service (INS) granted asylum to a homosexual based on a claim of persecution that involved sexual orientation. José Garcia (not his real name) was an illegal Mexican immigrant in the United States for ten years before he applied for asylum. Garcia said that as a young man in Coahula, Mexico, he was arrested by local police for walking in some neighborhoods, being in certain bars, and attending certain parties. Garcia also claimed to be the victim of both threats and rape at the hands of the police. While the INS ruling is not binding on other immigration officers, it should help to establish a precedent, or legal reason for later action, for similar cases.[9]

Seeing the Relationship of Old and Young in Perspective

In Chapter 6 you read that although young and old people have some different interests, they are both members of one

The Reverend Jesse Jackson leads this 1993 gay and lesbian rights march on Washington, D.C. in 1993. While progress has been made, gays and lesbians are still fighting for equality in all facets of society.

community. In this society, traditionally people help one another, knowing that others will help them, too, when the occasion arises. Yet this traditional cooperation has been challenged by some people as a result of economic problems that the United States has faced in the recent past.

One way the cooperation between old and young has been expressed is in our Social Security system. Under Social Security, workers have some of their pay deducted for Social Security taxes. That money is invested in U.S. Treasury bonds. Then, when a person retires, usually around the age of sixty-five, he or she can start receiving Social Security benefits based on how much was earned during that person's working years. Generally, whoever has worked at least ten years may receive Social Security benefits. Benefits are also periodically raised to take account of the rising cost of living. Social Security benefits are not taxed unless the person receiving the benefits, though above retirement age, is working and making over a certain amount of money.[10]

But Social Security is not only a retirement program. In fact, retirees make up only 60 percent of Social Security recipients. Three other groups—workers with disabilities, dependents of Social Security recipients, and the surviving spouse or children of someone who has died—are also eligible to receive Social Security benefits. In fact, about forty million people of all ages, almost one out of every six Americans, collect some kind of Social Security benefit. Part of the Social Security tax also goes to cover Medicare, which is the country's health insurance program for those over sixty-five and for many of the disabled.[11]

The Social Security system works smoothly as long as the benefits received by retirees and other Social Security recipients over time do not greatly decrease the overall funds in the Social Security trust. However, when there is (1) high inflation, (2) fewer workers entering the job force, or (3) a much larger number of retirees, then increases in the Social Security tax or other adjustments are made to correct the system.

During the 1970s and 1980s, and to some extent in the more recent past, at least two of the three above conditions have been present. As a result, Social Security taxes have increased, not only to pay for increased benefits for today's elderly, but to prepare for the decades ahead when a much larger number than usual of retired workers from the post World War II baby-boom generation will be eligible to receive benefits.

Some people have used these facts to argue that the old should pay more for their benefits in order to lighten the burden on the young. These people propose freezing cost-of-living increases on Social Security benefits, requiring wealthy senior citizens to pay more for Medicare, and taxing all Social Security benefits, whether or not the individual is working, just as private pensions are taxed.[12]

Many elderly people respond that while occasional adjustments in the Social Security system are necessary, it is wrong to suggest that the Social Security system sets one generation against another. As you have already read in Chapter 6, Social

Security benefits both old and young. Second, without Social Security, the poverty rates among the elderly would increase from 15 percent to about 50 percent. Also, the whole long-term basis of Social Security is that the money workers put in today they will get back later with full account taken for increases in the standard of living.[13]

Does the present Social Security system discriminate against younger workers? The question is probably too complex to rate a simple answer. But any answer that fails to recognize the close mutual dependence between old and young required by the Social Security system can hardly be expected to solve the problems that the question has raised.

The Future of People with Disabilities

As we learned in Chapter 3, the 1964 Civil Rights Act banned discrimination against blacks, women, and ethnic and religious minorities. In passing the Americans with Disabilities Act (ADA), Congress has stated, in effect, that people with disabilities also deserve their share. The civil rights movement of the 1960s, however, was much more effective at raising the consciousness of the public about racial justice than the movement for people with disabilities has been in dramatizing their own rights. As a result, we may be moving toward a period in which public opinion, still largely ignorant of people with disabilities, could backlash.

In fact, a poll released in the fall of 1991, a year after the passage of the ADA, but before it took full effect, found these attitudes about those with disabilities:

- 92 percent usually admired them.

- 74 percent felt pity for them.

- 47 percent felt fear because they, too, could have a disability at some point.

- 16 percent felt anger "because people with disabilities are an inconvenience."

- 9 percent felt resentment because of the "special privileges people with disabilities receive."[14]

The same poll found that only 18 percent of those questioned were even aware of the ADA. The ADA was a surprise even to many people with disabilities themselves, because they were so used to hearing other people's excuses for not accommodating them.

Yet in specific towns and cities across the nation people with disabilities are fully integrated into society. Talladega, Alabama, for example, has been described in one newspaper as one "user-friendly city for disabled people." About one thousand of the town's nineteen thousand citizens have disabilities. Half of these are students at the Alabama Institute for the Deaf and Blind, which also includes facilities for those with multiple disabilities.

Talladega has adapted to people with disabilities in a number of ways. Talking stoplights guide pedestrians. The local McDonald's provides menus in Braille. Video shops have sign-language tapes and movies captioned for the hearing-impaired. Church services are conducted in sign language.

A number of blind and/or deaf people work at a local factory, run by the institute, that makes paper products, neckties, mops, and other items. People with disabilities account for at least 75 percent of the factory's production. One newspaper described the operation as a "striking example of how disabilities can be overcome...."[15]

It is clear that American society still has a long way to go before its citizens with disabilities reach the level of acceptance that they do in places such as Talladega. But with these models, as well as the example set by people such as Marilyn Hamilton, and with the leadership of corporations such as IBM, Marriott, and McDonald's, the vision of a society with full inclusion of people with disabilities is gradually becoming a reality.

The Fight Against Discrimination Is in Your Hands

Will the future bring a society in which there is more segregation and conflict among different ethnic, racial, and other groups? Richard Lamm, former governor of Colorado, thinks so. He has written about his vision of that society in *Megatraumas*, published in 1985. In Lamm's scenario, Hispanic Americans become such a large part of the U.S. population that they demand their own nation in the Southwest. A newly powerful Ku Klux Klan plays an important role in starting a movement against immigrants. The economy is unable to create enough jobs for its own citizens, let alone for the hundreds of thousands of

A multiracial crowd of all ages filled New York City on June 20, 1990 to watch a parade in honor of Nelson Mandela's fight for freedom in South Africa. Role models like Mandela, who endured twenty-seven years in prison for his beliefs, have inspired others to continue the fight against discrimination in all of its forms.

immigrants—legal and illegal—who swamp the United States. Cities become minority ghettos, "social time bombs" surrounded by white suburbs.[16]

Lamm did not, however, foresee new immigration laws designed to control illegal immigration. Nor did he anticipate either the North American Free Trade Agreement (NAFTA), whose passage will likely make for better relations with Mexico, or the decline in the power of the Ku Klux Klan, thanks to organizations such as the Southern Poverty Law Center.

Will the future bring a stronger, multiracial society that draws strength from its very diversity? Such a scenario is projected by Henry Cisneros, Secretary of Housing and Urban Development in 1994 under President Clinton. Writing in 1988, Cisneros sketched a scenario in which the new immigrants to the United States, mostly Hispanic Americans and Asian Americans, offer two key elements:

1. A younger outlook on life than that of the relatively older and white population.
2. A strong commitment to the American dream that hard work and sacrifice can lead to great rewards.

Out of the cultural mingling of traditional ethnic values—emphasizing family, compassion, and sharing—and American rationalism and drive to succeed in the new economy, Cisneros sees a new and richer American culture emerging. His main concerns in realizing this vision are these:

1. The need for educating the growing minority population.

2. The need for economic growth, especially among the lowest income groups.

3. The need for innovative ways of building consensus and cooperation among the many culturally diverse groups that are now recognized.[17]

Which view of America's future do you see coming to pass: An America that is weakened or strengthened by the struggle and dialogue between different groups?

Will discrimination against minority groups play a more or less important role than it does now?

What can you do so that you and your friends will grow up in a society where people do not merely accept those who are different from them, but also learn to enjoy and cherish the differences as well as the similarities between themselves and others?

The choice is in your hands.

Chapter Notes

Chapter 1

1. Neil E. Lewis, "Rejected as Clerk, Chosen as a Justice: Ruth Bader Ginsburg," *The New York Times,* June 15, 1993, p. A1.

2. "Ex-Eagle Scout Sues Over Ban on Homosexuals," *The New York Times,* July 30, 1992, p. A12.

3. "Boy Scouts to Allow Homosexuals in New Program," *The New York Times,* August 14, 1991, p. A12.

4. Richard Aquila, *Rock and Roll: A Chronicle of an Era, 1954-1963* (New York: Schirmer Books, 1989), pp. 356–357.

5. Richard B. Schmitt, "Teen Discrimination," *The Wall Street Journal,* July 14, 1993, p. B5.

Chapter 2

1. Susan and Daniel Cohen, *When Someone You Know Is Gay* (New York: M. Evans, 1989), p. 57.

2. "Reported AIDS Cases Among Heterosexuals Growing at Faster Rate," *The Wall Street Journal,* March 11, 1994, p. B5.

3. Peter White, *Disabled People* (New York: Gloucester Press, 1988), p. 5.

4. Gunnar Myrdal, *An American Dilemma: The Negro Problem and Modern Democracy* (New York: Harper, 1944), pp. 75–76.

5. Ibid., p. 76.

Chapter 3

1. 26 Federal Register 5184 (1961). Quoted in Trudy J. Hanmer, *Affirmative Action: Opportunity for All?* (Hillside, N.J.: Enslow Publishers, 1993), p. 17.

2. *World Almanac and Book of Facts* (New York: Pharos Books, 1992), pp. 448–449.

3. Southern Poverty Law Center study, as reported in *Jet*, March 9, 1992, p. 25.

4. John Dovidio, "The Subtlety of Racism," *Training and Development*, April 1993, p. 53.

5. Ibid., pp. 53–54.

6. Geoffrey Smith and Mike McNamee, "There's No 'Whites Only' Sign, But...," *Business Week*, October 26, 1992, p. 78.

7. Ibid.

8. Constance Johnson, "Policing Its Own Ranks," *U.S. News & World Report*, September 20, 1993, pp. 37–38.

9. Phillip Hoose, *It's Our World, Too! Stories of Young People Who Are Making a Difference* (Boston: Little, Brown, 1993), pp. 17–25.

10. Benjamin A. Holden, "Parent of Denny's Restaurants, NAACP Agree on Plan to Boost Minorities' Roles." *The Wall Street Journal*, July 1, 1993, p. A3.

11. Stephen Labaton, "Denny's Restaurants to Pay $54 Million in Race Bias Suit," *The New York Times*, May 25, 1994, p. A1.

12. Geraldine Woods, *Affirmative Action* (New York: Franklin Watts, 1989), p. 18.

13. Poll was conducted by Louis Harris for the Center for the Study of Sport in Society at Northeastern University and the Reebok Foundation. Quoted in Richard Lapchick, *Five Minutes to Midnight: Race and Sport in the 1990s* (Lanham, Md.: Madison Books, 1991), pp. 224, 229.

14. Mark Starr, "Baseball's Black Problem," *Newsweek*, July 19, 1993, pp. 56–57.

15. Anti-Defamation League flier, "A World of Difference Objectives," undated.

16. Ibid.

17. Ibid.

18. Ibid.

19. Quoted in Marjorie B. Green, "Making A World of Difference," *School Safety,* Fall 1991, pp. 10–11.

Chapter 4

1. Dr. Nan Stein, director of the Sexual Harassment Project at the Wellesley College Center for Research on Women. Quoted in Lawrence Kutner, "Harmless Teasing, or Sexual Harrassment?," *The New York Times,* February 24, 1994, p. C11.

2. Trudy Hanmer, *Taking a Stand Against Sexism and Sex Discrimination* (New York: Funk & Wagnall's, 1990), p. 10.

3. Ibid.

4. Rhona Mahoney, "Car Buying: Why Women Get a Lemon of a Deal," *Ms. Magazine,* January-February 1991, p. 87.

5. Louise Derman Sparks, "Empowering Children to Create a Caring Culture in a World of Differences," *Childhood Education,* Winter 1993/1994, pp. 67–68.

6. Michael Marriott, "Hard-Core Rap Lyrics Stir Black Backlash," *The New York Times,* August 15, 1993, p. A42.

7. Shari Roan, "Negative Images?," *Los Angeles Times,* August 18, 1992, pp. E1, E4.

8. DeNeen L. Brown, "Some Area Girls Find Discrimination Lingers," *The Washington Post,* February 12, 1992, p. A8.

9. American Association of University Women, "How Schools Shortchange Girls," Referred to in Mary Jordan, "Wide Gender Gap Found in Schools," *The Washington Post,* February 1, 1992, p. A1. Research from this report is also included in Myra and David Sadker, *Failing at Fairness: How America's Schools Cheat Girls* (New York: Scribner's, 1994).

10. Ibid., p. A8.

11. "Sex Discrimination? It Happens Only to Others, Many Women Say," *The Wall Street Journal,* January 25, 1994, p. A1.

12. Jordan, p. A8.

13. Ibid., pp. A1, A8.

14. Chester E. Finn, Jr., "Biased Against Everyone," *American Spectator,* June 1992, p. 37.

15. Millicent Lawton, "Girls Will and Should Be Girls," *Education Week,* March 30, 1994, p. 25.

16. Kevin Sullivan, "Bethesda Student Has Long Had the Strength to Speak Out," *The Washington Post,* August 4, 1992, p. B1.

17. Stephen Buckley, "Montgomery's Girl Athletes Face Inequalities, Panel Finds," *The Washington Post,* December 15, 1992, pp. A1, A8.

18. Sullivan, p. B7.

19. Linda Greenhouse, "Court, 9-0, Makes Sex Harassment Easier to Prove," *The New York Times,* November 10, 1993, pp. A1, A22.

20. Ibid., p. A22.

21. Echo Montgomery Garrett, "How to Avoid Scalping at the Hair Salon or Barbershop," *Money,* August 1993, p. 16.

22. M.F. Thompson, "Why Women Pay More than Men for the Same Services," *Mademoiselle,* March 1993, p. 92.

23. Ibid.

Chapter 5

1. Eric Schmitt, "Pentagon Must Reinstate Nurse Who Declared She Is a Lesbian," *The New York Times,* June 2, 1994, p. A1.

2. Janice E. Rench, *Understanding Sexual Identity* (Minneapolis, Minn: Lerner, 1990), p. 17; Rachel Kranz, *Straight Talk About Prejudice* (New York: Facts on File, 1992), p. 87.

3. Judith Newman and Sarah Skolnik, "Speaking Out," *People Weekly*, November 29, 1993, p. 129.

4. Susan and Daniel Cohen, *When Someone You Know is Gay* (New York: M. Evans, 1989), pp. 57, 61–63. In April 1993, a sex survey conducted by the Battelle Human Affairs Research Center found that only 1 percent of men twenty to thirty-nine years old described themselves as exclusively gay, and only 2 percent said that they had a homosexual experience in the last ten years. However, as Richard A. Isay, M.D., noted in a letter to *The New York Times*, April 25, 1993, p. E16, "Neither homosexual behavior nor self-acknowledgment is an accurate indicator of who is homosexual," because both sexual behavior and sexual desire are often inhibited in our society.

5. Walter Isaacson, *Pro and Con: Both Sides of Dozens of Unsettled and Unsettling Arguments* (New York: Putnam's, 1983), p. 142.

6. "Homosexual rights movement." *Encyclopedia Britannica*, 15th Edition (New York, Encyclopedia Briticannica, 1991, vol. 6), p. 31.

7. "Reported AIDS Cases Among Heterosexuals Growing at Faster Rate," *The Wall Street Journal*, March 11, 1994, p. B5.

8. Bob Cohn, "Discrimination: The Limits of the Law," *Newsweek*, September 14, 1992, p. 38.

9. Bill Turque, "Gays Under Fire," *Newsweek*, September 14, 1992, p. 39. For the direct quotation and the figure of thirty-one cities, see Arthur S. Leonard, letter to the editor, *New Yorker*, July 25, 1994, p. 6.

10. Cohn, p. 39.

11. Ibid., p. 36.

12. M.T. Saghir, E. Robins, and B. Walbian, *Male and Female Homosexuality* (Baltimore, Md.: Williams & Wilkins, 1973). Quoted in "Factfile: Lesbian, Gay, and Bisexual Youth" (New York: Hetrick-Martin Institute, 1992), unpaged.

13. Ibid.

14. E.S. Hetrick and A.D. Martin, "Developmental Issues and Their Resolution for Gay and Lesbian Adolescents," *Journal of Homosexuality*, 14(1/2): 1987, pp. 25–43; quoted in: "Factfile: Fighting the Myths: Lesbians, Gay Men—and Youth" (New York: Hetrich–Martin Institute, 1993), unpaged.

15. Lindsey Gruson, "Meeting Gay Bias Face to Face in Class," *The New York Times*, October 15, 1993, p. B13.

16. "The Hetrick-Martin Institute," pamphlet published by the institute, undated.

17. Jesse Green, "This School Is Out," *The New York Times Magazine*, October 13, 1991, p. 36.

18. Chris Bull, "Group's Survey Says Hate-Crime Reports Rose in Six Areas," *The Advocate*, April 9, 1991, p. 14.

19. Ibid., p. 15.

20. Joseph P. Shapiro, "The True State of Gay America," *U.S. News & World Report*, October 19, 1992, p. 39.

21. Eloise Salholz, "The Future of Gay America," *Newsweek*, March 12, 1990, pp. 24–25.

Chapter 6

1. Marilyn Webb, "How Old Is Too Old?," *New York*, March 29, 1993, pp. 68-69.

2. Guy Halverson, "Older Workers Shine in Study of Performance," *Christian Science Monitor*, May 24, 1991, p. 9.

3. Paul Thorne, David West, and Ron Owen, "The Case for Salvaging the 'Throwaway' Executive," *International Management*, May 1987, p. 49.

4. Ibid.

5. Ken Wibecan, "Highlights: People," *Modern Maturity,* August-September 1992, p. 14.

6.Leslie Lindeman, "Beating Time," *Modern Maturity,* June-July 1991, pp. 28, 34.

7. Terri Thompson, "Experience Not Wanted: Job Cuts Are Growing, and So Will Age-Discrimination Suits," *U.S. News & World Report,* December 30, 1991, p. 59.

8. Thomas J. Lueck, "Job-Loss Anger: Age Bias Cases Soar in Region," *The New York Times,* December 12, 1992, p. A50.

9. Melinda Beck, "Old Enough to Get Fired," *Newsweek,* December 9, 1991, pp. 64, 66.

10. Lueck, p. A50.

11. Udayan Gupta, "Age Discrimination Guidelines Adopted by New York City," *The Wall Street Journal,* November 18, 1993, p. B9.

12. Howard Gleckman, "Social Security's Days as a Sacred Cow Are Numbered," *Business Week,* April 2, 1990, p. 33.

13. Horace B. Deets, "Young and Old, We Are One People," *Modern Maturity,* April-May 1991, p. 9.

14. Jerrold Berkson and Shirley A. Griggs, "Intergenerational Understanding in the Middle School," *Educational Digest,* April 1987, pp. 30–32. Originally appeared in *The School Counselor,* November 1986, pp. 140–143.

15. Marc Freedman, "Fostering Intergenerational Relationships for At-Risk Youth," *Children Today,* March-April 1989, p. 12.

16. Ibid., pp. 12–13.

Chapter 7

1. Joseph P. Shapiro, *No Pity: People With Disabilities Forging a New Civil Rights Movement* (New York: Times Books, 1993), p. 211.

2. Carolyn Wiley, "Programs That Lead the Way in Enabling People With Disabilities to Work," *Employment Relations Today,* Spring 1992, p. 32.

3. Charlene Marmor Solomon, "What the ADA Means to the Nondisabled," *Personnel Journal,* June 1992, p. 73.

4. Shapiro, pp. 211–214.

5. Ibid.

6. Ibid., p. 165.

7. Ibid., pp. 165–167.

8. Susan Chira, "When Disabled Students Enter Regular Classrooms," *The New York Times,* May 19, 1993, p. A17.

9. Ibid.

10. Shapiro, p. 175.

11. Wiley, p. 33, quotes an unemployment figure of 58 percent for all men with disabilities and 80 percent for all women with disabilities, as of 1990, citing as the source R.L. Thornburgh, "The Americans with Disabilities Act: What It Means to All Americans," *Labor Law Journal,* December 1990, p. 805.

12. Catherine Yang, "Business Has to Find a New Meaning for 'Fairness,'" *Business Week,* April 12, 1993, p. 72.

13. Wiley, p. 32.

14. Thomas D. McLaughlin, "Accommodating the Disabled," *Management Accounting,* November 1992, p. 35.

15. Yang, p. 72.

16. Shapiro, pp. 145, 147.

17. Ibid., pp. 147–148.

18. Ibid., p. 148.

19. Wiley, p. 35. This information first appeared in R.A. Lester and D.W. Caudill, "The Handicapped Worker: Seven Myths," *Training and Development Journal,* August 1987, pp. 50–51.

20. Ibid., pp. 35–36.

21. Ibid., p. 37. This information first appeared in J.J. Laabs, "The Golden Arches Provide Golden Opportunities," *Personnel Journal,* July 1991, pp. 52–54.

22. Solomon, pp. 73, 78.

23. Yang, p. 72.

Chapter 8

1. Juan Williams, "The New Segregation," *Modern Maturity,* April-May 1994, pp. 28, 30.

2. Ibid. p. 28.

3. Douglas S. Massey and Nancy A. Denton, *American Apartheid: Segregation and the Making of the Underclass* (Cambridge, Mass: Harvard University Press, 1993). Quoted in Williams, p. 32.

4. Kevin D. Thompson, "Back to School," *Black Enterprise,* November 1990, p. 56.

5. Ibid.

6. Steven A. Holmes, "Some Employees Lose Right to Sue for Bias at Work," *The New York Times,* March 18, 1994, p. A1.

7. Ibid.

8. Linda Greenhouse, "Court Opens Path for Student Suits in Sex-Bias Cases," *The New York Times,* February 27, 1992, pp. A1, A16.

9. "Gay Man Who Cited Abuse in Mexico is Granted Asylum," *The New York Times,* March 26, 1994, p. A5.

10. U.S. Department of Health and Human Services, *Understanding Your Social Security,* Social Security Administration, Pub. No. 05-10024, January 1992, p. 10.

11. Howard Gleckman, "Social Security's Days as a Sacred Cow Are Numbered," *Business Week,* April 22, 1990, p. 33.

12. Ibid.

13. William R. Hutton, "The Young and the Old Are Not Enemies," *USA Today*, March 1989, p. 65.

14. Louis Harris & Associates, Inc., Public Attitudes Toward People With Disabilities, conducted for National Organization on Disability. Quoted in Joseph P. Shapiro, *No Pity* (New York: Times Books, 1993), pp. 328–329.

15. Tony Horwitz, "Talladega, Alabama, Is a User-Friendly City for Disabled People," *The Wall Street Journal*, February 14, 1994, p. A1.

16. Quoted in William Dudley and Bonnie Szumski, eds., *America's Future: Opposing Viewpoints* (San Diego, Calif.: Greenhaven Press, 1990), p. 282.

17. Henry Cisneros, "The Demography of a Dream," *New Perspectives Quarterly*, Summer 1988. Reprinted in Dudley and Szumski, pp. 272–277.

Where to Write

RACIAL DISCRIMINATION

Anti-Defamation League
(nationwide organization: see area
telephone book for local chapters)

One Lincoln Plaza, Suite 301
Boston, MA 02111
(617) 330-9696   FAX (617) 439-6033

Center for the Study of Sport in Society
Northeastern University
300 Huntington Avenue, Suite 161CP
Boston, MA 02115
(617) 373-4025

Educators for Social Responsibility
475 Riverside Drive, Room 450
New York, NY 10027
(212) 870-3318

**National Association for the
Advancement of Colored People (NAACP)**
4805 Mt. Hope Drive
Baltimore, MD 21215
(410) 358-8900

Southern Poverty Law Center
400 Washington Avenue
Montgomery, AL 36104
(205) 264-0286   FAX (205) 264-3121

GENDER DISCRIMINATION

American Bar Association (ABA)
1800 M Street NW
Washington, DC 20036
(202) 331-2200

National Organization for Women (NOW)
1000 16th Street NW, Suite 700
Washington, DC 20036-5705
(202) 331-0066

National Women's Political Caucus
1275 K Street NW, Suite 750
Washington, DC 20005
(202) 898-1100

DISCRIMINATION AGAINST GAYS AND LESBIANS

American Civil Liberties Union (ACLU)
132 West 43 Street
New York, NY 10036
(212) 944-9800

Hetrick-Martin Institute
401 West Street
New York, NY 10014
(212) 633-8920 FAX (212) 989-6845

Lambda Legal Defense and Educational Fund, Inc.
666 Broadway, 12th floor
New York, NY 10012
(212) 995-8585

National Gay and Lesbian Task Force
1734 14th Street NW
Washington, DC 20009
(202) 332-6483

Gay and Lesbian National Crisis Line
(800) 889-5111

AGE DISCRIMINATION

American Association of Retired Persons (AARP)
601 E Street NW
Washington, DC 20049
(202) 434-2277
1-800-453-5800

Equal Employment Opportunity Commission (EEOC)
1801 L St NW
Washington, DC 20036
(202) 663-4264

Foster Grandparents
2500 Martin Luther King, Jr. Avenue SE
Washington, DC 20020
(202) 678-4215

The Gray Panthers Project Fund, Inc.
1424 16th Street NW
Washingon, DC 20036
(202) 387-3111

National Council of Senior Citizens
1331 F Street NW
Washington, DC 20004
(202) 347-8800

DISCRIMINATION AGAINST PEOPLE WITH DISABILITIES

Children's Defense Fund
25 E Street NW
Washington, DC 20001
(202) 628-8787

Disability Rights Education and Defense Fund
2212 6th Street
Berkeley, CA 94710
(510) 644-2555

Glossary

abstinence—Refraining from sexual intercourse.

affirmative action—The taking of active steps by an organization to seek out minority and women job applicants.

AIDS—Acquired Immune Deficiency Syndrome is a progressive, degenerative disease affecting several major organ systems, especially the immune system and central nervous system. AIDS is caused by the human immunodeficiency virus (HIV).

American Association of University Women (AAUW)— It was founded in 1881 to work for the advancement of women through lobbying with emphasis on lifelong learning. A separate AAUW foundation supports fellowships, research, and public service projects.

Americans with Disabilities Act (ADA)— Legislation passed in 1990. It prohibits discrimination against those with disabilities in employment, public services, and accommodations, such as large stores, buses, and trains.

anthropologist—A scientist who studies the origin, physical and cultural development, biological characteristics, customs, and beliefs of human beings.

Anti-defamation League (ADL)— A group founded in 1913 to stop the destruction of the reputation of the Jewish people, to secure justice and fair treatment for all citizens alike, and to promote interfaith relations.

autism—A mental condition marked by extreme self-absorption or withdrawal from reality.

bias—The tendency to favor one side of an issue over another.

binding arbitration—A technique used in labor problems in which employer and employee agree to abide by the decision of a judge selected by both sides.

bisexual—A person who is sexually attracted to members of both sexes.

cerebral palsy—A disability marked by lack of coordination in the muscles and speech disturbance.

culture—The sum total of the ways of living developed by a group of human beings and transmitted by them from one generation to another.

curriculum—A course of study; material included in such a course.

demagoguery—The practice of stirring people by appealing to their emotions and prejudices.

disability—The condition of being unable to participate fully in at least one major life activity because of illness or injury.

discrimination—Unjust treatment of an individual or group based on prejudice about the group to which that person belongs.

empathy—The ability to experience the feelings of another person.

Equal Employment Opportunity Commission (EEOC)— An organization created by the Civil Rights Act of 1964. It enforces government laws that counter discriminatory acts against minorities as they affect employment. The Commission has the power to conduct investigations, make judgments based on the evidence gathered, attempt to bring opposing parties into agreement, and file lawsuits.

gay—A male homosexual.

gender—Identification as male or female.

gender discrimination—Unjust treatment of a person solely because of his or her gender.

hate crime—A crime committed against an individual or group because of race, religion, ethnic origin, gender, or sexual orientation.

heterosexual—A person who is sexually attracted to members of the opposite sex.

HIV—The Human Immunodeficiency Virus that causes AIDS. HIV is transmitted through blood, usually by intimate sexual contact, contaminated needles, or from an HIV-positive mother to her unborn child.

homosexual—A person who is sexually attracted to members of the same sex.

institutional racism—The use of an established organization's power to favor one race over others.

lesbian—A female homosexual.

mainstreaming—The practice of placing children with special needs in regular classes.

muscular dystrophy—A hereditary disease in which muscles gradually waste away.

National Association for the Advancement of Colored People (NAACP)— An organization founded in 1909. Its aim is to improve the status of minority groups, to eliminate racial prejudice, to keep the public aware of the effects of racial discrimination, and to take action to eliminate such discrimination.

norm—A standard for a particular group; type, model, pattern.

paraplegic—A person who cannot move or feel from the waist down.

plaintiff—A person who begins a lawsuit.

precedent—An action or example that serves as a reason for a later action.

prejudice—A negative opinion or an opinion formed beforehand without knowledge, thought, or reason, that a person holds but does not necessarily express or act upon.

quadriplegic—One who has paralysis of both arms and both legs.

race—A group of human beings that is considered to have passed on certain physical traits from one generation to another.

racism—The belief that one race—usually one's own—is superior to other races.

rehabilitation—Restoration to a good condition.

retarded—Slow in mental development.

segregation—Separation of one racial or other minority group from another, especially in schools.

self-esteem—The valuing of oneself.

sexism—An attitude or behavior based on traditional stereotypes of gender roles.

sexual harassment—Repeatedly bothering or tormenting someone because of his or her gender. Specifically, unwelcome sexual advances made by an employer, superior, or co-worker, especially when they are made as a condition of continued employment or advancement.

spina bifida—Congenital disease in which the spine splits.

stereotype—A simplified or standardized mental picture of someone or something.

workers' compensation—The monetary payment to an employee for injuries that the employee suffered on the job. It is paid from insurance purchased by the employer.

Further Reading

Bender, David L. and Bruno Leone, eds. *American Values*. San Diego, Calif.: Greenhaven Press, 1989.

Cohen, Susan and Daniel. *When Someone You Know Is Gay*. New York: M. Evans, 1989.

Dudley, William, ed. *Racism in America: Opposing Viewpoints*. San Diego, Calif.: Greenhaven Press, 1990.

Dudley, William, and Bonnie Szumski, eds. *America's Future*. San Diego, Calif.: Greenhaven Press, 1990.

Gay, Kathlyn. *Bigotry*. Hillside, N.J.: Enslow Publishers, 1989.

Hanmer, Trudy. *Affirmative Action: Opportunity for All?* Hillside, N.J.: Enslow Publishers, 1993.

—-. *Taking a Stand Against Sexism and Sex Discrimination*. New York: Funk and Wagnalls, 1990.

Hoose, Phillip. *It's Our World, Too! Stories of Young People Who Are Making a Difference*. Boston: Little, Brown, 1993.

Isaacson, Walter. *Pro and Con: Both Sides of Dozens of Unsettled and Unsettling Arguments*. New York: Putnam's, 1983.

Kranz, Rachel. *Straight Talk About Prejudice*. New York: Facts on File, 1992.

Kuklin, Susan. *Speaking Out: Teenagers Take On Race, Sex, and Identity*. New York: Putnam's, 1993.

Mizell, Linda. *About Racism*. New York: Walker, 1992.

Myrdal, Gunnar. *An American Dilemma: The Negro Problem and Modern Democracy*. New York: Harper, 1944.

Sadker, Myra and David. *Failing at Fairness: How America's Schools Cheat Girls*. New York: Scribner's, 1994.

Salzman, Marian, and Teresa Reisgies. *150 Ways Teens Can Make a Difference*. Princeton, N.J.: Peterson's Guides, 1991.

Shapiro, Joseph P. *No Pity: People with Disabilities Forging a New Civil Rights Movement.* New York: Times Books, 1993.

Steele, Shelby. *The Content of Our Character: A New Vision of Race in America.* New York: St. Martin's Press, 1990.

Swisher, Karin, ed. *The Elderly: Opposing Viewpoints.* San Diego, Calif.: Greenhaven Press, 1990.

Terkel, Studs. *Race: How Blacks and Whites Think and Feel About the American Obsession.* New York: New Press, 1992.

Walls, David. *The Activist's Almanac: The Concerned Citizen's Guide to the Leading Advocacy Organizations in America.* New York: Simon and Schuster, 1993.

Woods, Geraldine. *Affirmative Action.* New York: Funk and Wagnalls, 1989.

Index